Climates of Tragedy

Climates of Tragedy

By

William Van O'Connor
WITH THE ASSISTANCE OF
Mary Allen O'Connor

NEW YORK
RUSSELL & RUSSELL · INC
1965

REISSUED, 1965, BY RUSSELL & RUSSELL, INC.
BY ARRANGEMENT WITH LOUISIANA STATE UNIVERSITY PRESS
L. C. CATALOG CARD NO: 65—13951

PRINTED IN THE UNITED STATES OF AMERICA

To

Robert Penn Warren

Acknowledgments

For permission to use quotations I am indebted to:

Maxwell Anderson for lines from his plays and from the *Essence of Tragedy,* Allen Tate and the Princeton University Press for passages from *The Language of Poetry,* Simon and Schuster for sentences from John Cowper Powys' *Enjoyment of Literature,* W. H. Auden for lines from *The Ascent of F–6,* Harcourt Brace for brief matter from I. A. Richards' *Principles of Literary Criticism* and lines from T. S. Eliot's *Murder in the Cathedral* and *Family Reunion,* Charles Scribner's for passages from George Santayana's *The Realm of Spirit* and "Tragic Philosophy" as well as for lines from Allen Tate's *Reactionary Essays,* Kenneth Burke and the Louisiana State University Press for a passage from *Philosophy of Literary Form,* Robert Sherwood for brief passages from several of his plays, Cleanth Brooks for lines from *Modern Poetry and the Tradition,* and Robert Penn Warren for a passage from an unpublished address.

Preface

If the text of this study were four or five times its actual size there would be less need for such a justification as this. Frequently I have wanted to fill in with convincing illustrations and saving qualifications. To do this, however, would have been to destroy the original purpose of the study: to indicate the chief philosophical attitudes that have obtained, and must obtain, in eras of dramatic tragedy. And, conversely, to sketch briefly some of the philosophical attitudes that are death to tragedy. The aim has not been to evolve a definition of tragedy, but to present a theory of philosophical patterns (the phrase is Professor W. C. Curry's) in which the tragic spirit conceivably may have inhered. This task would hardly have needed doing if a better understanding of Periclean Greece and Elizabethan England were the desired end. I cannot hope to add to the scholarly refinements on refinements. Evaluations of the intellectual currents in these two periods in contrast to other periods in Western history are important, however, if in the process we can see what has prevented the creation of tragedy in our age, and what hope there seems to be for dramatic tragedy.

The length of consideration, therefore, given to various themes in this study is best understood if it is seen that a clearer view of the backgrounds of contemporary drama, in those areas that border on tragedy, is being striven for. In the first section of the study some signposts are erected, so that the reader can be prepared for themes that I consider important in the pattern of tragedy and for my personal "biases." Such a theme as the "Vision of Evil" might be investigated at almost infinite length—but for my purpose here an indication of its significance, and one chief illustration thereof, must suffice. The treatment of the tragic protagonist as an individualist who through personal speculation and suffering reaches both a keen awareness and spiritual resiliency is important as a partial statement of the nature of tragedy and particularly as a statement of a significant contemporary problem and its effect on tragedy. Little space is given to the effects of romanticism on tragedy because this theme has been frequently studied, and, secondly, it is of relatively slight importance in contemporary drama. Slightly more space is given to the effects of supernaturalism on contemporary drama chiefly because one of our major poets, steeped in the drama of Greece, and searching for a moral order, has tried to give body to his drama by leaning on the faith of his fathers. The effects of naturalism on our drama have been considered more fully for the obvious reason that the very life and pulse of recent serious drama has been dependent on this spirit. The use of three such all-covering terms is hardly to be avoided, if even greater ambiguities of expression are to be side-stepped. Poetic diction, it may seem, has been unduly stressed. Yet if one considers that diction is not to be thought of in terms of simple metrics, but as an alembic of philosophical attitudes of a poet and his age then such a treatment is doubly justified. Finally, an effort has been made to catch up a few strands that will enable one to roughly evaluate contemporary efforts to write dramatic tragedy.[1]

Once again I must emphasize that the seemingly glib nature of my generalizations is not the re-

[1] This final section is a rewriting of "The Rebirth of Tragedy," *Shakespeare Bulletin,* XII (Apr., 1941), 16.

sult of wilful carelessness—most of them are commonly accepted generalizations and all of them are made thus briefly because of the danger of forgetting, in looking at a piece, the appearance of the entire mosaic. Surely, with the commonly emphasized need for synthesis in literary fields some such tentative probing as this is necessary. That fuller developments and varied interpretations of stated themes are still needed and that new themes are yet to be suggested and worked out I should emphasize most carefully. Perhaps I have done my part in giving at least a point of departure.

This little volume was, in a sense, written against a deadline. While in pursuit of the elusive spirit of Melpomene, I was ever aware of the "unperturbed pace" and "deliberate speed" of Mars in pursuit of me. Although I cannot ask the reader's indulgence for any ill-considered statements, the kindest reader may not consider it amiss if I mention that these pages were written during moments between the fulfillment of academic duties. Apparently I had to choose between writing it after the war and telescoping the doing of it into the very few months preceding military service.

I am indebted to Professor Cleanth Brooks and to Professor John Olive for their helpful comments on the manuscript and to Professor T. A Kirby, who examined the chapter on poetic diction prior to my reading it before the Louisiana College Conference. The usual last-sentence-bow toward one's wife this time is not a mere pleasantry for she has eyed and evaluated the entire study sentence by sentence in its making; indeed some of the themes were suggested by her and the directions they take are almost invariably the result of our arriving at a common critical agreement.

WILLIAM VAN O'CONNOR

Hartford, Conn.

Contents

Climates of Tragedy

ONE can readily enough accept Max Förster's theory that the psychological differences in literary or historical periods are the result of what he calls "'polar reaction' in the human soul,"[1] even though one cannot accept his characterizations of such periods. The attitude of various eras toward religious faith, toward the amount of freedom and indulgence granted the individual, toward science, toward the fact of death, toward *joie de vivre,* toward the nature of poetry, toward . . . , will differ radically.

Given a man with poetic powers and intellectual awareness the attitudes of various ages toward these philosophical concepts will allow of or of necessity preclude his creation of dramatic tragedy. To discover the component concepts that must inhere in a climate that nurtures tragedy one can

[1] "The Psychological Basis of Literary Periods," *Studies for William A. Read,* 254–268.

turn to Greece and Elizabeth's England. In both realms one discovers similarities in predispositions, proclivities and tolerances. In grouping and analyzing likenesses and dissimilarities in the two periods many of the basic elements of tragedy come into brighter prospect. A more "practical" result is come by when contemporary tolerances are set side by side with those of the earlier periods. If our era is or is not to produce dramatic tragedy we will do well to discover the dissimilarities in our communal mind and those of Elizabethan England and Periclean Greece—and therefore in our theatres.

The importance of individualism in an age or state that would willingly produce dramatic tragedy can hardly be overstated. In Greece and in Elizabethan England the individual was allowed a relatively free range. The very term Renaissance has become synonymous with personal freedom—and, too often, license. Max Förster has, in an unhappy generalization, called the age from 1500–1900 the "Age of Individualism." Even a cursory glance at this period will indicate that the term "individualism" cannot be so readily applied. His noncharacterizing term "New Age" for the period from 1900 on, of course, hints nothing at the struggle for and against individualism that is going on.

Natural impulses within a commune will work to drag down beneath its staid surface any individual whose tone or work offends the commonality. But no recent period in Western history has seen such an unabashed race toward collectivism. And one does not have to limit such comments to the followers of ideologies who blatantly ask for such a levelling. If a glance at individualism in Greece and Elizabethan England indicates serious defects in our society one at least is this: individualism has been either unrestricted or all but totally repressed. There has been no sustained effort to cultivate restricted individualism, that in its flowering rises above mind to spirit. Dramatic tragedy has not flourished in any other soil.

Certainly an era must be keenly aware if its people would attempt to understand their relation to the universe. They must be willing to move constantly toward new intellectual peaks, to throw off vacuous clichés, and the too easy explanations of some orthodox religionists. Only thus are new and fuller moralities evolved. The intellectual curiosity and philosophical solutions of the world of Sophocles do not have to be labored: we still turn to them. The intellectual revolution that is the modern world, begun in the Renaissance, drew its sustenance in part from Greece. These later Europeans, in a manner similar to that of the Greeks, took a further departure in becoming concerned largely with the generalizations to be drawn from considerations of "irreducible and stubborn facts." The partially new morality that is discovered in Hamlet can be nothing less than a reflection of these further reaches of the mind. A yet further move may be hoped for after one ponders the significance of such an observation as this of Professor Max Lerner: "The intellectual revolution of the twentieth century is likely to prove the charting of the *terra incognita* of the irrational and the extracting of its implications for every area of human thought." [2] Our theatre already may have worked a good way through the throes of these psychological problems. The next step—on the part of the society rather than on the part of the dramatist—is yet to be seen.

Protagonists of the mind, men who in freedom seek to understand themselves, must come early upon a hard truth: that they live in a world of irrationalities, that their very minds tend downward into the natural sea of unconsciousness, that tragedy is born of the struggle toward rationality. Thus

[2] This passage is taken from the title essay in *Ideas Are Weapons.*

the awareness of evil. But this awareness does not remain static.

Soon some discover that there are ways to hide from evil—and a move to engender optimism is underway. Innumerable theories are evolved—that goodness must prevail, that nature is good, that science will cure all ills—and for a time a society can avoid facing the fact of permanent evil. Facets of evil, such as the fact of death, are glossed, avoided, misinterpreted in the interest of mental comfort. Yet some ages, those in which tragedy has flourished, have learned that a "profound realization" is the key to a keener awareness of life. Some of the concepts we have come to indicate by the terms romanticism, supernaturalism, and naturalism represent the attitudes of periods, or individuals, which have failed to attain this "profound realization."

The romantic mind finds it difficult to be satisfied with generic qualities; it inclines toward exaggeration. In one direction, romanticism moves away from serenity toward excess in color, movement, and hope; in another, toward an almost preternatural tranquillity. The latter area of romance merges with certain forms of supernaturalism in its denial of the need or worth of human activities and probings; the former area merges with the tragic vision but escapes into its own realm when restlessness and violence overweight the balance and calm achieved in tragedy. In periods that have glorified and striven for the romantic view the expression of tragedy has been all but impossible.

Our contemporaries find it difficult to read, other than as historical documents, certain of the dramas of Aeschylus, Sophocles, Euripides, and even Milton. The dogmas of theology, based on posited religious truths and on revelation, seem divorced from the mind nurtured and fed on the beliefs discovered in the drama of humanism, in which man alone is the chief concern. The struggle of early Greeks to free themselves from blood ties that spelled irrationality and death is interesting as record, but hardly as a situation to experience vicariously. Those dramas in which the gods interfere and thus wilfully change the course of human action are likewise too difficult to accept in a world that emphasizes individual responsibility. Even that doctrine that posits the belief that fortune rests in the hands of a benevolent deity—to which man owes the obligation of service and obedience—is too reassuring to allow man to discover his strength within himself.

In ages that lack the courage to press back against the intense "pressure of reality" naturalism inevitably arises. The long-drawn-out suffering man endures, the abnormalities he sees, the pettiness he witnesses prevent his envisioning man in his potential greatness and dignity. Again, the spirit of criticism—legitimate in its own realm—tends to lessen the poet's capacity for seeing life broadly, as he must in tragedy. Preoccupation with relatively minute—however important—problems tends to destroy perspective and, concurrently, to depress the observer. In the short view, surely, man is ignoble. Whatever the cause of naturalism, the dramatist discovers the partial truth it contains. This portion, he finds, is easily encompassed. He needs no broad vision, and can find his material under his hand. He is concerned with observables. When the spiritual strength of a people declines, when it fails to rise above the pressure of fact and circumstance naturalism shortly obtains.

Paradoxically, prolonged human misery and the tragic spirit are antithetical. Human happiness heightens our appreciation of the tragic spirit. Joyous comedy and stark tragedy are never far apart. The sad-eyed Egyptians thought the Greeks—who delighted in games and pageants—"such children."

If we have come to think of Renaissance England as a daily "Costume Ball" it is that the record the Raleighs, the Shakespeares, the Dekkers, the Campions have left us is a composite of adventure, song, love, and joy. And next it, tragedy. Two songs, one from the sixth century B.C., the other of Shakespeare's, reflect the same delight and the same sense of the transiency of all delights.

We, like the leaves of many blossomed spring
When the sun's rays their sudden radiance fling
In growing strength, on earth, a little while,
Delighted, see youth's blooming flowerets smile.
Not with that wisdom of the Gods endued,
To judge aright of evil and of good.
Two Fates, dark-scowling, at our side attend;
Of youth, of life, each points the destined end,
Old age and death: the fruit of youth remains
Brief as the sunshine scattered o'er the plains. . . .[3]

That time of year thou may'st in me behold
When yellow leaves, or none, or few, do hang
Upon those boughs which shake against the cold,
Bare ruin'd choirs, where late the sweet birds sang.
In me thou see'st the twilight of such day

[3] Trans. by C. A. Elton from Mimnermus.

As after sunset fadeth in the west,
Which by and by black night doth take away,
Death's second self, that seals up all in rest.
In me thou see'st the glowing of such fire,
That on the ashes of his youth doth lie,
As the death-bed whereon it must expire,
Consumed with that which it was nourish'd by.
This thou perceiv'st, which makes thy love more
strong,
To love that well which thou must leave ere long.

One can hardly say that the best of our poetry is usually much more than tentative intellectual probings. Like our art, composed mainly of experimental angles and planes, our poetry is too often mathematical when it is not debasingly naturalistic. We have yet to make both an intellectual *and* emotional synthesis of joy and grief.[4] "Every man," says Keats,

. . . whose soul is not a clod
Hath visions, and would speak, if he had loved,
And been well nurtured in his mother tongue.

[4] I have not given separate consideration to the espousal of life and to the *de contemptu mundi* themes as they affect tragedy. The themes are more than adequately treated by Willard Farnham in *The Medieval Heritage of Elizabethan Tragedy*.

An age is most readily seen for what it is in its poetry. Its sense of human dignity, its awareness of evil, its intellectual insight, its susceptibility to shibboleths, its efforts to understand itself—whatever feelings and thoughts are floating in the "latent dream" force themselves to the surface. A society that produces dramatic tragedy must, of necessity, possess a combination of qualities that result in this particular philosophical attitude and literary genre; for tragedy presupposes a selection of certain disparate experiences and attitudes which being woven together artistically create a rare illusion of reality at its most exquisite moments. To adequately examine an era's poetry is to discover its innermost hopes, illusions, and despairs. The poetry of irony, with its implication that the writer has not succumbed to the cheapness of falsely-fed hopes or to the emotional debauchery of despair is discovered a chief element in the poetry of the tragedians of both great eras and also of the best of contemporary poets. And in the efforts of these same poets to refuse to moralize or propagandize in verse there is further indication of basic sincerity, as there is a lack of it in the verse of the consciously didactic writers of all eras. When poetry loses, as it has in various ages, its hard intellectual basis and "gains" the easily understood word, the easy generalization—the prosaic—dramatic tragedy is gone. The move that is likely to occur in reaction to simple statement in poetry will be in the direction of a poetry clouded by a romantic haze, the intellectual core of which is discovered upon investigation to be mushy. The eras that have cultivated didacticism, easy generalizations, romantic mistiness in their poetry are conspicuously lacking in dramatic tragedy. There is yet another facet. An age that writes its poetry—however sincerely—in a stark, unlovely language offends at the other extreme. Beautiful lines, musically lovely, sensuously suggestive of odor, color, or touch, were set side by side with stark lines, and metaphysical complexities in Shakespeare. Tragedy, an "all-ordering, all-accepting experience," can hardly reflect its complexities in using a diction that narrowly reflects a single theory of poetry.

The Vision of Evil

When the late Roman world denied the existence of evil there was no further possibility of tragedy. The tragic protagonist agonizes that he may bring good out of evil. Only the exceptional soul, among an exceptional people, can endure the requisite sufferings. It is an affirmation of nobility, an implicit statement that man does not have to recoil from malign and mysterious forces.

Since truth is protean and elusive, man tends to seek answers, even unsatisfactory answers, if he is spared the obligation of searching for the right questions. Even such brilliant questioners as Euripides tire of looking for key questions and satisfy themselves with seemingly remediable problems. It is to be expected that the heroic probings of Aeschylus would degenerate into the sophisticated and cleverly ironic barbs of an Aristophanes.

It is at this point presumably that man declines to find his strength in himself. The Greek tragedian saw evil as discoverable, his later imitators as apparent no doubt but as inexplicable. The next step is to deny the evil itself. Reason has discovered rationalization.

Without attempting to note the various components that make up the Christian synthesis one may state that Christianity offered her own explanation of the problem. Christianity did not, of course, deny evil: she offered supernatural aids to counterbalance its effects.

With the coming of pure tragedy in the Renaissance the arc is completed and another is begun. The tragedian of necessity leaned on inherited beliefs regarding the nature of evil but the exploration of it, as observed in tragic protagonists, has again become a personal quest.

The Renaissance, it is to be inferred, had an intense awareness of evil, and actively considered a number of philosophical and theological theories of the nature of evil. William Bradley in his *Shakespearean Tragedy* interprets the core of the tragic world to be a moral order. Evil forces—hatred between families in *Romeo and Juliet,* Iago in *Othello,* ambition and malice in *Macbeth*—disrupt the moral order and bring suffering and death. Evil feeds on goodness. This is the tragic fact. Without exquisite awareness of evil, therefore, there can be no dramatic tragedy.

It may seem obvious that such an awareness of evil is prerequisite to tragedy, and it is obvious. Yet there have been times and there are places in which the evil principle is seen neither as irreparable nor as man's chief problem. Whatever its cause, optimism—rationalized from hope in science, or because evil is often ignored when there is any fear of personal emotional disturbances—is destructive of tragedy.

The optimism generated by the seventeenth century is seen in little in Restoration tragedy. One most significant difference exists between the "heroic drama" of the Elizabethan and Restoration theatres: the Elizabethans were fascinated by evil, the Restoration writers were intent on the necessity of personifying goodness. Restoration tragedy is, in large part, the story of great passions—but always "virtuous passions." This progeny of dramatic failures—if we are looking for tragedy—cannot be re-outlined here.[1] A second remark of Bonamy Dobrée's is, however, pertinent as well to contemporary drama: "[N]o art can be really great which does not accept humanity for what

[1] See *Restoration Tragedy.*

it is. The moment it tries to guide mankind into channels, or endeavors to prevent its being mankind, an essential element is omitted. . . . [T]he great statement of tragedy . . . is what happens to man. . . . For in tragedy it is the spectacle of man pitting himself against the inevitable which is moving." An art of escape, rather than of "profound realization" is chimerical and romantic.

Some of the dominant philosophical theories of the eighteenth century would seem to be responsible for the complete absence of tragedy in the period. The neoclassicists and deists were pretty well agreed that the universe was a closed system, a completely interlocking arrangement. If man could discover the inter-relationships he might set aside evil. Ultimately then there was no irrevocable evil in the universe. Further, such concepts as poetic justice, the theory of benevolence, the doctrine of plenitude, "sentimentality," all worked toward nullifying the grim recognition of permanent protean evil.

To take an example: although David Hume is considered a great world figure in philosophy, his essay "Of Tragedy" is an easily recognizable piece of the eighteenth century mosaic. It is hardly exaggeration to say that some of his sentences might flow readily enough from the lips of Tristram Shandy's Uncle Toby if not from those of his unbelievable father. The substance of tragedy as understood by Hume is a warm soft mash:

The heart likes naturally to be moved and affected. Melancholy objects suit it, and even disastrous and sorrowful, provided they are *softened by some circumstances.*

He is not satisfied to let anguish remain anguish:

We weep for the misfortune of a hero to whom we are attached. In the same instant we comfort ourselves by reflecting that it is nothing but a fiction: And it is precisely that mixture of sentiments which composes an *agreeable sorrow,* and tears that delight us.

A sentence from Professor Cleanth Brooks is appropriate here: "All serious literature including tragedy, of course may be regarded as a sort of make-believe; but the furious, deadly serious make-believe that is drama was [by the end of the eighteenth century] dead." Hume, we may infer, was in accord with his contemporaries' view of the world as a "vast and ordered mechanism" and of man as good, "actuated by benevolence toward all mankind and toward all creatures." Tragedy in its essence is thus denied and turned into a thing of delight. It would seem a fair generalization then to say that as the Elizabethan world has receded so has the Vision of Evil—at least until quite recently.

W. B. Yeats recognized a spirit of optimism in Emerson and in Whitman and concluded that they must ultimately "seem superficial, precisely because they lack the Vision of Evil." Emerson believed in law and order as an absolute and in disorder as only "a phenomenon." And he came to believe all sorrow "superficial." To Emerson "pure malignity" could not exist. In the face of Hawthorne and Melville one can hardly hold Emerson up as *the* symbol of his era. He does however seem to reflect his age more fully. Presumably then it is to our glory that more recent poets—T. S. Eliot and Yeats, for example—have accepted the "inevitable co-existence of good and evil in man's nature, . . ." and "possess the power to envisage some reconciliation between such opposites." [2]

We have seen how many inheritors of this op-

[2] F. O. Matthiessen, *American Renaissance, passim.*

timism reacted to new discoveries of evil within themselves. Quite naturally, Sigmund Freud's explanation of man's shadow-side, and the discovery of the filth that resides (consciously or unconsciously suppressed) in man's mind caused violent opposition to his school. Yet Freud's discoveries were the most effective antidote possible for ungrounded optimism about the potential greatness of mankind. It bespeaks only blindness in the observer to deny the shadow and to see only the light. To become so obsessed with the filth in the human being that the nobility goes unnoticed is, on the other hand, to confess a narrow, nonmetaphysical vision.

Quite possibly the failure of the nineteenth and the twentieth centuries to be concerned with the fundamental problem of permanent evil is the faith that has obtained in the powers of science, and, by a strange transfer, in the powers of the social "sciences." The attitude of society toward science has not yet come full circle. Those with even a slightly Wellsian cast to their minds still feel that there is little in the seemingly irrational universe that cannot be straightened out. John Strachey, for example, has gone so far as to say that after science has straightened out the social order, it can straighten out the individual. The painful fact that the social-minded forget is this: no good comes into the world without a corresponding evil. Technology, organization—science—have granted boons, rapidly and extensively; and technology, organization—science—have brought catastrophic evils just as rapidly and just as extensively. Evil may be hydra-headed, and many specific evils may be rectified, but the corrections do not destroy the source of the evil.[3]

Such criticism cannot be levelled, however, at the most intellectually aware contemporary poets.[4] In fact, a passage in *Family Reunion* is a criticism of the same optimism and refusal to face evil that we have already indicated:

[3] Perhaps the failure of much contemporary literature to approach the tragic view is to be inferred from these words of Robert Penn Warren who, in an unpublished address, repeated an Italian journalist's explanation of the popularity of Faulkner in Italy: "Faulkner is important to us because he understands that there is such a thing as evil. He is a barbarian, and that may be the reason he still believes in evil. But that is the reason he is great. We Europeans are not barbarians; we no longer believe in evil. We see great evils, we see this war, but we believe that those evils can all be corrected in political and military and economic terms. Both Fascism and Communism are against the Church, because the Church maintains that evil exists. Both Fascism and Communism hold that you only have to correct specific evils."

[4] For examples, see W. H. Auden and Christopher Isherwood, *The Ascent of F-6*, *passim*, and Robert Penn Warren, "Original Sin," *Eleven Poems*.

We all of us make the pretension
To be the uncommon exception
To the universal bondage. . . .

We only ask to be reassured
About the noises in the cellar. . . .

Hold tight, hold tight, we must insist that the
world is
What we have always taken it to be.

Rightly enough Nietzsche wrote that the absence of evil would take away the function of the tragic poet. So, too, of course, does an age's refusal to consider evil for what it is destroy tragedy. And, if the chief thread in the pattern of evil—death—were abolished, writes Theodore Spencer, "our conceptions of comedy and tragedy, our ideals of bravery, of beauty, of wisdom, our views of others and of ourselves," would all be changed. Death is an aspect of evil that, at first thought, it would seem difficult to misunderstand, but some have managed even this.

AND ITS CENTRAL ASPECT: DEATH

The early Christian thought in terms of a Celestial City, of death as the gateway from the unimportant to the all-important,—from death to life. We think of Paul, of Augustine, of the Church fathers in terms of repressions of the body and of the natural man; we think of the Egyptian in terms of vast monuments to the dead. "To the Egyptian the enduring world of reality was not the one he walked in along the paths of every day life but the one he should presently go to by the way of death." [5]

The Greeks were realists in the better sense of this abused word. They did not soften life "by sentimentalizing it." Professor Hamilton has said: "It was a Roman [and the Romans had no true tragedy] who said it was sweet to die for one's country. The Greeks never said it was sweet to die for anything. They had no vital lies." [6] The Greeks' joyful consciousness of life sharpened their awareness of death. Even Clytemnestra, the Lady Macbeth of Greek drama, in the *Agamemnon* of Aeschylus withdraws in disgust from unnecessary killing. To Aegisthus, her paramour, and to the Chorus she says:

Nay, enough, enough, my champion! We will
smite and slay no more.

[5] Edith Hamilton, *The Greek Way,* 12.

[6] *Ibid.,* 83.

Already have we reaped enough the harvest field of guilt:
Enough of wrong and murder, let no other blood be spilt.
Peace, old men! and pass away unto the homes by Fate decreed;
Lest ill valor meet our vengeance—'twas a necessary deed.
But enough of toils and troubles—be the end, if ever, now
Ere thy talon, O Avenger, deal another deadly blow.

When life lost its zest for the Greeks the tragic muse departed. This is seen in watching the metaphysical questionings of Plato come to a negative answer in the "skeptical attack" of Pyrrho—he who was willing to give up exhilaration for tranquillity. He saw death as he saw life, as neither a certain good nor a certain evil. One should accept all things calmly: there was nothing else to do. Stoicism, partially the pagan counterpart to Christian Calvinism and Puritanism, likewise taught that man must not defy; rather, he must accept. Death had no sting: "the soul survives the body, but only as an impersonal energy. At the final conflagration the soul will be reabsorbed, like Atman into Brahman, into that ocean of energy which is God." In such thoughts the way of the Orient may be seen in victory over the way of Greece. The coming of Rome was then possible, even inevitable. Life had become quiescent; death a half-desired Nirvana.

Late classical philosophers—neo-Platonists, who all but identified evil with material things; the Stoics, who strove to ignore worldly feelings—plowed the field that was to be sowed by the early Christians. This life, taught some of the followers of Christ, was important only as a preparation for eternal delights; death should be anticipated as the supreme moment of one's life, not its unhappy conclusion. Then for centuries, points out Professor Theodore Spencer, works were written on death, works which "are a collection of abstractions." Gradually, though, considerations of death came to be "in deadly emotional earnest."

Ded is the most dred thing that es in all this world.[7]

A considerable time before the writing of this work, back, indeed, as far as the twelfth century,

[7] *Pricke of Conscience, cir.* 1340.

artists had begun a realistic treatment of Christ and the Virgin.[8] The abstractions of Christianity became the flesh and blood family of Joseph, Mary, and the Christ Child. "This appeal to emotion by an attempt at realistic portrayal of the objects of emotion marks more than anything else the first steps of the Renaissance. . . ." [9] Soon people were, in the light of Christ's sufferings and death, contemplating their own deaths. By the fourteenth century artists had pushed realism to an extreme—the decomposing bodies of the dead became the morbid interest of the saint, preacher, poet, and common man. By the fifteenth century the figure of death—the skeleton—had evolved; it obtains to this day. The latter part of the century was "frenzied about death." [10] And true tragedy was but a century away.

During the first half of the sixteenth century the orthodox contemplation of death is to be found in hundreds of verses, but the mundane order, particularly under the rich velvet coverings of Elizabeth's court, found a renewed emphasis.

[8] For a full treatment of the Cult of the Virgin, its connections with art, etc., see Henry Adams, *Mont Saint Michel.*

[9] Theodore Spencer, *Death and Elizabethan Tragedy,* 15.

[10] See B. P. Kurtz, *The Dance of Death and the Macabre Spirit in European Literature.*

Thus with a background of wealth, stimulating and glamorous living, life became more and more desirable. Death became the courtier's not-to-be-forgotten Nemesis.

"Dismally death's injurious approaches sap the beauty and wit of woman and man's strength and glory. Reconcilement to the fatal necessity, and a seemly end are the most that can be effected. The motive and energy of *Measure for Measure* is in the horror of being dead, which is by no means overcome by the incomparable reflections on the nothingness of life with which the Duke fails to convince Claudio, who simply cannot bear to die." [11] Claudio speaks without rant, in measured words:

> The weariest and most loathed worldly life
> That age, ache, penury and imprisonment
> Can lay on nature is a paradise
> To what we fear of death.

But it is in Hamlet that the conflict burns most intensely. He gives great promise intellectually, socially,—his life should be lived gloriously. Sud-

[11] H. O. Taylor, *Thought and Expression in the Sixteenth Century,* II, 258.

denly, he loses faith in the courtly life, he reverts, as though affected by an atavism, to the fearful thoughts, dressed in the refinements of the most recent philosophical speculations, of death that had haunted the generations behind him. Nowhere perhaps are the paradoxes of the mind to be seen more vividly: the Elizabethan audience feared death, yet they were fascinated at witnessing the deaths of characters on the stage. To lose the things of this world, to die, was *tragedy*.

In the tragedies of the Elizabethan era death is met defiantly, courageously. This is tragic dignity, an acceptance of death born of an acceptance and appreciation of life. Innumerable stories—from Sir Thomas More's death down to the lopping of heads under James I—bear witness to the calm and perception of irony exhibited by condemned Englishmen. Audiences that witnessed such scenes at the gallows and block could have had no difficulty in seeing their counterpart on the stage.

Perhaps several running generalizations on the late seventeenth century and the eighteenth century attitude toward death in literature—keeping in mind some few of the fluxes and mutations in intellectual currents—will serve to indicate partially, at least, the absence of tragedy in this era.

Sentimentality is one way in which to lessen one's intellectual awareness of evil. Demand, for example, that stories end pleasantly, and the appreciation of the inexorable nature of death is sidestepped. Nahum Tate saw a greater propriety in keeping Lear and Cordelia alive, and so changed the ending of *King Lear* to suit this belief. The nature of the heroic plays—their concern with characters and situations exaggerated beyond possible acceptance, their obviously fictional emphasis—makes it easy for the auditor to consider death as represented therein as occurring in an unreal realm. Again, the preoccupation of the graveyard school of poets with death was ghoulish and morbid. One can hardly identify himself with mouldering corpses, food for worms. The shudder was for its own sake—not for what death signified to the keenly alive human being. Later developments of the romantic spirit took man even farther from appreciation of the fact of death, to "profounder" rationalizations.

There is as "stubborn dualism" [12] in the thought of Shelley as there was in that of his spiritual father, Plato. Shelley strained to see the "tower beyond tragedy," his glass was the doctrine of Plato:

[12] B. P. Kurtz, *The Pursuit of Death.*

"To his way of thinking, once the larger spiritual reality could be accepted, the smaller matter of the fate of the individual could be taken on trust. Fear of death, indeed, arises very largely from narrow contemplation of self; by consecrating our thoughts to interests beyond self, we diminish the minatory power of death." [13] In *Adonais* Shelley's doctrine of death discovers poetic liberation for a brooding, yet hopeful mind. Into a "last weighty stanza is compressed the pagan, unmitigated tragedy of the finality of death for the human individual":

Whence are we, and why are we? Of what scene
The actors or spectator? Great and mean
Meet massed in death, who lends what life must
  borrow.
As long as skies are blue, and fields are green,
Evening must usher night, night urge the morrow,
Month follow month with woe, and year wake year
  to sorrow.

There follows slow transition, horror lessens and, in phrases as beautiful as sunlight, a new vision, in a "poem of recantation," illumines the reader's mind:

[13] *Ibid.*, xiv.

Nor let us weep that our delight is fled
Far from these carrion kites that scream below;
He wakes or sleeps with the enduring dead;
Thou canst not soar where he is sitting now.
Dust to dust! but the pure spirit shall flow
Back to the burning fountain whence it came,
A portion of the Eternal, which must glow
Through time and change, unquenchably the same.

"Even the old anathema of tyranny and bigotry suffers a sea-change into a thing of dream and unreality:

'Tis we, who, lost in stormy visions, keep
With phantoms an unprofitable strife,
And in mad trance strike with our spirit's knife
Invulnerable nothings.

To such an unreality have dwindled the cordilleras of evil that agonized Prometheus! All these Adonais has outsoared in death, all the 'envy and calumny and hate and pain.' "[14] Shelley, the romantic, lifts his eyes over reality. Beautiful as his vision—

Life, like a dome of many-coloured glass,
Stains the white radiance of Eternity,—

[14] *Ibid.*, 275–277.

may seem to be, Shelley has retreated from the world of facts and actualities. Much as he would have disliked the associations, his answer to the tragedy of death is the same, though with a different ultimate belief, as that preferred by Theresa, John of God, or Francis of Assisi. As Indian mystics retreat from reality into the land of shadow, so does Shelley. *Adonais* is a "primitive faith," beautiful, yet an idyllic retreat; more sophisticated than the ancient Hebraic view of the Celestial City, yet on the same road, a few dreams beyond.

We have said that as the Renaissance world has receded, so too has the Vision of Evil; so, too, has the Vision of Death. Fallacies, such as this of Hazlitt, have served to lessen awareness: ". . . if we only cherish a fondness for existence according to the good we derive from it, the pang at parting with it will not be very severe!" Another indirect escape can be seen in Browning's "Prospice":

> Then a light, then thy breast,
> O thou soul of my soul! I shall clasp thee again,
> And with God be the rest!

This refusal to look squarely at death, to see it as the curtain against which all acts are performed takes away from the intensity and hard outlines of the acts themselves. Perhaps the contemporary world has too often prettied, when it has not evaded, the fact of death. Even the words—"mortuary park," "our dear departed," "passed away" —we use are euphemisms that prevent, or tend to, the realization of the starkness of death. This wilful refusal to see death in its unalterable awfulness must make a sudden personal awareness of death shocking to the point where "the whole child-universe fall[s] to pieces."

Perhaps, however, the words of Pericles, as repeated by Kaarlo in *There Shall Be No Night,* is a good augur of a desire to cut the husks of sentimentality and euphemism away from the realization of death: ". . . [Pericles] told the mourning people that he could not give them any of the old words which tell how fair it is to die in battle. . . . Congratulate yourselves that you have been happy during the greater part of your days. . . ."

The Tragic Protagonist

THE INDIVIDUAL AND THE COMMUNE

UNDERSTANDING, or if one will, spirit, may be thought of as the moral focus of an individual born of the reaction of the psyche to the "ambient forces" about it. At some stage in his development man discovered forces within himself that were incompatible with the ideals his understanding presented to him. With heavy fingers and eyes unaccustomed to close observation he began to tease the edges and to probe toward the core of his own nature. He discovered differences between himself and the man who had not paused to look within himself. He learned that instinct inclines us away from problems, from rationality. Nature would solve the problems for her child, but her conscious child does not necessarily believe in the wisdom of her decisions. Understanding, however, being no absolute tool for reordering nature, sees devious paths of action. Therein is indecision. Awareness has issued man an invitation to tragedy. Yet the more courageous intellects have the pride or reason that forbids a return to nature, to unconsciousness.

Man, in his history so far, has chosen to struggle against a return to the unconscious collectivism of primitive existence. Indeed, the process has moved man toward a rationale that glorifies the individual at the expense of the mass. The problems of the individual in conflict with society's needs have moved some few psychologists to belief in the desirability of conditioning individuals for a well-defined niche in society. This they would call Utopia. Aldous Huxley has reminded such neglectors of spiritual values what would happen in a "perfectly conditioned" society. In the social scheme of *Brave New World* characters are conditioned from birth away from all desires for individuality, for unique personalities. The "Savage" versed in Shakespeare could not make his conditioned literary friend understand why Romeo should want to die simply because he finds Juliet dead. Helmholtz, the literary friend, says upon hearing portions of *Romeo and Juliet* read, "And who's going to get excited about a boy's having a girl or not having her?" Ironic it is that rationality can, even in an imagined ideal commonwealth, reach the point where it destroys itself. If such a society were to come to pass the cycle of conscious man would have come full circle: rational man would have chosen to offer up his mind, sharpened by the buffets that inevitably come to a unique personality, to the sluggish comfort resident in minds that know no conflicts. The collective mind would have triumphed, the individual would have sacrificed himself to the "good" of the mass. Nature would have tricked conscious man into unwitting self-betrayal.

Yet to blindly decry the shortsightedness of those who would delight in the society of *Brave New World* is to see only one side of the medal, that whereon the clean strength, the intellectual intensity, and unique beauty of the individual is displayed. There is another side. To allow the individual an unrestricted radius wherein to move and yet to prevent his completely disrupting the sphere about him is a delicate problem. Only a balance between mind and spirit can make for integration of the individual and the group and for the spiritual enlargement of the individual. Once the individual asserts his "rights" the old ease of sacrificing the one to the many is changed to a tragic conflict. We will remember the death of Iphigenia —and the response of Clytemnestra. Extreme individualism and chaos are parts of the same syllogism. Yet to sacrifice the individual is to sacrifice the things of the spirit—to sink hazily back into the tellurian surges and subsidings of the collective mass, to lose the hope of rational advances. Individualists in Greece learned, for a time, to maintain this balance.

The stateliness of tragedy, the doctrine of self-control that staid classical scholars attribute too strongly to the Greek have tended to hinder our seeing Athenian life as a society of vigorous individualists. Certainly no comic writer has ever been more alive to personality than Aristophanes. The lives of Athenians were full: there was a feverish delight in discussion, a fervent belief that bodies were to be used, an almost frivolous gaming and sense of competition. Their desire to know and understand, and their faith in man's ability to chart the heavens was parcel of their individual inquisitiveness and versatile interests. Pericles said the "individual Athenian in his own person seems to have the power of adapting himself to the most varied forms of action with the utmost versatility and grace." The point does not have to be labored. "Here is faith in life and man, a zest for living never rivaled again until the Renaissance."

Only such a society could have been electrically caught up at witnessing the mazes through which Oedipus was, with the utmost self-assurance, stalking his way. This man, this confident, intellectually aware simpleton—why couldn't he see! This was an individualist—the Athenians, aware of irony, could appreciate him. This sense of the Athenian's individual importance, Herodotus has written, had come quite suddenly—when they had shaken off the yoke of the dictators. Their spirits were their own.

In looking at the tragedy of Greece in contrast with the tragedy of Shakespeare we too often say that fate destroys the Greek protagonist and personal weakness the Shakespearean protagonist. This is not quite true—but it is an indication of a difference in the two eras. The protagonist in Shakespeare tends to become the play, the protagonist in Greek tragedy more often symbolizes, and is a relatively small but very significant part of the tragic pattern. Greece did not sacrifice the individual—such varied conceptions of the same historical figure could not have been delineated if this had been so. She learned, for a time at least, to use the individual as the vanguard of her collective spirit. In the short period of this balance, science, art, philosophy, and literature marked a golden age. When the individual was destroyed by the collective group, the dissolution of Greece was a galloping consumption.

The denial by the Jews of Christ's doctrine of the importance of the individual was the collectivist voice of the East crying down the most disturbing of ideas—that one man, among his millions of fellows, is unique, a temple not made by hands. Like the Greeks, Christ taught a counterbalance, but whereas the Greek saw the relationships between individuals in a society (mind) and also saw the need for cultivating the power in the individual (spirit) Christ taught the individual should deny himself when the needs of his brothers became apparent. The effect on the individual would, in both instances, be much the same: there would be greatness in simplicity, for the individual would have no need to develop in freakish directions—his greatness lay in reflecting, in simple beauty, the greatness of the universal.

Unlike Christ, many early Christians, driven

within themselves by persecution, denied the individual his right to growth. All things not of the invisible world were as nothing. The same forces that had denied the individual in the East were leavening in the West. The extremes of this evil could not obtain for long, but for a time it was as though Socrates had not lived. The movements toward individuality within the medieval commune may be visualized as a great system of pendulums: the largest and most indicative of the era had swung in the direction already suggested; others, relatively much smaller moved in either direction, even sometimes winning a temporary interest. Generally, however, we have to envision a new background, the Renaissance, before we can think of the pendulum as having swung, all but too far, to the other side.

One thinks first of the characters Macbeth, Lear, Hamlet, Richard II, not of the plays they are a part of. The complexities, fullness and depth of their personalities cause these characters to overflow their dramatic parts. It seems inevitable, considering the emotional and intellectual power these plays have, that the characters would overflow: certainly the almost childish nature of the stories themselves could not explain such permanent and intense interest. That the rise of the individual in this era is no mere textbook cliché is borne witness to in the lives of sixteenth century Englishmen—philosopher to swashbuckler.

The Tudor and particularly the Elizabethan individualist usually had a capacity (or perhaps he faced a necessity) of combining exquisite awareness of the world he lived in with an adventurous, daring physical life. From vain young Surrey, intellectually alert and intensely alive, to Sidney, sober, reflective and yet willing to fight if obliged to, to Raleigh and Essex, both as sharply cognizant of intellectual currents as of dangerous political intrigues, Renaissance England reflects an acceptance of individualism hardly less significant than that of Italy. The court was peopled with incisive-minded men, courageous, and zealous for full personal development. Philosophers like Bruno were court guests; literary geniuses often lived out of the purses of courtiers; adventurers like Raleigh could raid Spanish libraries for the filling of English bookshelves. It is not incongruous to turn from the romantic, intellectually alive men of this age to the romantic and equally aware tragic protagonists of Shakespeare.

From our vantage point in the twentieth century we can look back wistfully at the figure of Hamlet, conceived in terms of spirit that is understanding, and less wistfully at the self-portrait of Cellini, self-assertion gone wild. A more stable society, less given to glorifying individuals six times their normal size, could have prolonged and strengthened the advances of an era to which we still look for sustenance. There is little point in numbering those who parted the skies in hopes of seeing new spaces. Enough that the collective mind was strong enough to draw these figures down beneath the conventional surface. They were honored as memories, but their like were not welcomed for generations to come.

Milton's hope in the Christian Utopia in essence is this: if poets, as well as social and moral philosophers, would submit tentative beliefs and doctrines for general evaluation, in time a mosaic of truth could be pieced together. Fulfillment of his ideal meant a society, religious and social, that had evolved a collective security. Granting the possibility of such an evolution, only a static society could be achieved. And such a society would mean, even presuming some improvements, a throwback to the Ptolemaic and ordered system desired by so many in medieval Europe. New cries would have been heard that such and such an action was "against Nature," that such and such an attitude meant a wilful dislocation of a God-ordained order. The *modern,* the man who foresees possible advances, would be thwarted and persecuted. *Moderns* would be looked upon as subversive, heretical. A norm once achieved, no progress would be possible. No dramatic tragedy could be created in this imagined "Utopia," for no auditor could glory in the strength of a tragic protagonist opposing an irrational social or universal order. It is not too much to attribute, in part at least, the failure of the Enlightenment to produce dramatic tragedy to the era's preoccupation with establishing "uniformity" as the desideratum.[1] These generations

[1] "That which is 'according to nature' meant, first and foremost, that which corresponds to this assumption of uniformity; it is perhaps still necessary to repeat that in the most frequent of the normative uses of the term 'nature' in the Enlightenment, the principal element in the signification of the word *is* uniformity. . . . Despite its sixty-odd other senses, it was primarily and chiefly because of this connotation that 'nature' was the sacred word of the Enlightenment. And the campaign of which it was thus the war cry, the general attack upon the *differentness* of men and their opinions and valuations, the quest of a universal point of view and the consequent apotheosis of the least common denominator of human nature—this with the resistances to it and the eventual revulsion against it, was the central and dominating fact in the intellectual history of Europe for two hundred years—from the late sixteenth to the late eighteenth century." A. O. Lovejoy, "The Parallelism of Deism and Classicism," *Modern Philology,* XXIX (Feb., 1932), 283.

after Shakespeare—despite their admiration for him—were unwittingly destroying a central doctrine of Shakespearean tragedy: Shakespeare would, as John Cowper Powys states, have declared "himself an individualist; one, that is to say, who finds in the character of the individual rather than in any collective or standardized 'ideology,' as we call it now, the chief redeeming element of the world and the best hope for the well being of humanity." [2]

The nineteenth century, after quickly stifling yells for personal freedom, settled down to a new era of conformity, not greatly unlike that of its heritage of two centuries. Ironically, a further move of the mind—expressed reverently as Science—neglected to consider the spirit of the individual. Aided by divers disillusionments man awoke one day to find he had become in his own eyes little more than an animated vegetable. If one knew enough formulae it was possible to do anything at all with the human mass. Unfortunately these same formulae reached the wrong hands—a new scientific society was envisioned, one in which the individual again was as nothing.

Although we have seen periods since the Renais-

[2] *Enjoyment of Literature,* 215–216.

sance during which the glories of individualism have been played down, the virus is still with us—and still growing. Now that we have the stage of several centuries to study it against, individualism is no longer seen as an end to ills. Mass susceptibility to suggestion, stupid misinterpretation, the choice of the banal and the crass is seen as a by-product of personal freedom. The dust stirred up by individual digging tempers our delight in personal freedom, even remembering that heroes are likely to be studied in retrospect and fools in close prospect. The value of individualism that results in spiritual personalities remains, however, the greatest of our cultural heritages.

Nicholas Berdyaev, for example, speaks of the spirit forming personality, transfiguring the "biological individual" and making him "independent of the natural order. . . . Conflict between good and evil or between any values can only exist for a person. Tragedy is always connected with the personality—with its awakening and its struggles." [3]

[3] *Destiny of Man*, 72.

AWARENESS AND DIGNITY THROUGH SUFFERING

Perhaps our own sensitiveness to personal suffering and, by extension, the pity we feel for suffering in others is the basis of the emotion we call love. This explains the auditor's deep personal concern with the sufferings of the tragic protagonist—it is the foundation of his sense of togetherness with the protagonist, for they are crushed beneath the same weights. The auditor is concerned with the same barriers to happiness, with the serenity that evolves from suffering borne with dignity, with the indestructible strength of man's spirit. The aware auditor sees the protagonist as another star in the dark of nothingness, the shadows they have both come out of and will one day slip back into. The light of the spirit is played into the abyss, and although it is a transient value it is all man has. Together they are sparks of consciousness. "I see that all of us who live are phantoms and an empty shade," says Sophocles. In loving the protagonist, in compassion for him the auditor glories in the spiritual warmth of a fellow creature shortly to be lost in the dehumanized unknown outer spaces. The suffering of the protagonist is that of the auditor; it is the quickener of the consciousness of both.

Through suffering one attains reflective self-consciousness, an awareness of human limitations. This, it seems, is prudence and understanding. Since a well-ordered universe with which man may be articulated is still in the offing, there is only one temporary value, spirit. It is the only part of man, pulled hither and yon in painful confusion, that is of an order and realm untouched finally by the forces of unreason. Yet spirit, beyond struggle itself, is increased as the body is twisted on its wheel of fire.

But not every wail that dies in a whimper, not every anguished cry silenced in death's kingdom, not every agonized scream can be caught up and maintained in the tragic realm. Tragedy is not concerned with the pain or the suffering, but with the dignity with which they are endured. There are no retreats for the tragic protagonist. Neither in madness nor in the self-absolution of confusion may he retreat. No single tremor is to be lost even in the "forgetfulness of sleepe." The truly tragic hero "will weep no more," he "will endure." The ecstasy is not to be shunned. At this height he is alone, unique and sufficient. This is tragic dignity.

The protagonist who in his suffering signifies the common lot of mankind is a tragic sufferer. (Not that all men possess themselves in suffering —but then, all suffering is not tragic.) He is a symbol of strength, of revolt, of spiritual resiliency. The quality of thinness in pathetic suffering is divorced from the quality of fullness in tragic suffering. In the one there is pain, sharp or dull, of the here and now; in the other there are cosmic overtones.

Tragedy is essentially noble reaction to suffering. The protagonist finds himself lost in a well of evil, with mysterious darkness about him. As the intensity of his suffering increases he becomes increasingly aware that his only forte is his own spiritual strength. It is his sole support in midst of hauntingly mysterious forces. In this way spirit "asserts a subtle mastery over the thoughtless forces of Nature. . . . In the spectacle of Death, in the endurance of intolerable pain, and in the irrevocableness of a vanished past, there is a sacredness, an overpowering awe, a feeling of vastness, the depth, the inexhaustible mystery of existence, in which, as by some strange marriage of pain, the sufferer is bound to the world by bonds of sorrow. . . . all the loneliness of humanity amid hostile forces is concentrated upon the individual soul, which must struggle alone. . . ." [4]

In the presence of these values rests the representative greatness in *Oedipus* and *Lear,* and in the absence of them the weakness of much contemporary drama. Man in tragic drama, if such is to come, must in suffering find his fulfillment, his, as Christ said, "coming to himself." Only in the strenuousness of combat with nature can man win a victory. Otherwise the victory is nature's, a victory

> . . . meaningless
> As wind in dry grass
> Or rat's feet over broken glass
> In our dry cellar.

Again, Eliot in his play *The Family Reunion* has said that through suffering one passes to the other side of despair; it is the only road to morality:

> Whatever you have learned, Harry, you must remember
> That there is always more: we cannot rest in being
> The impatient spectators of malice or stupidity.

[4] Bertrand Russell, "A Freeman's Worship," *Mysticism and Logic.*

We must try to penetrate to other private worlds
Of make-believe and fear. To rest in our own suffering
Is evasion of suffering. We must learn to suffer more.

Both José Ortega y Gasset and Thomas Mann have shown that liberality, which in one aspect makes for the refusal of too many to assert self-discipline, is at the root of our mad drive toward barbarism. The ineluctable end is a loss of culture, refusal of individual responsibilities, of personal moral discipline—and ultimately the succors of retreat into collectivism. The ages of individualism, restricted individualism, have taught us one thing—that spirit is man's sole abiding value. An age that contemns mind, which in its highest reaches is spirit, is seeking suicide.

Ironically, those who feel that in easing or even eliminating individual suffering they are aiding mankind are unaware that they are destroying man's chief road to consciousness. These "conditioners" of mankind are his chief enemies. Ultimately they destroy human dignity.

In such a state there will be no sense of inherited values. The mechanist will have won his complete victory. Today we can still appreciate the conversation of the poet with the mechanist. "Astronomically speaking," the mechanist said, "man is wholly negligible." "Astronomically speaking," the poet answered, "man is the astronomer." A contemporary audience, despite its tragic limitations, can be elevated in its human kinship with man the astronomer. If the mechanists win this total victory there will be no tragedy and no human greatness. There will be no poetic overtones to be heard in the word "human."

Sensible Gullivers have been in our day too often bound and refused personal spiritual enlargement. Powys has had the same thought in reading Montaigne: "When one turns the calm gaze of what might be called humanity's unsanctified *common sense* upon the world spread out before us today, with its bombings and shootings and murderous 'ideologies' and its ferocious hatred of all unregimented, unhypnotized free souls, it begins to appear as if Montaigne's sensuous-psychic *love of himself* and obstinate concern with himself were quite possibly going to prove the chief oracular word for the next great psychological reaction." [5] The importance to society of the strug-

[5] Powys, *Enjoyment of Literature*, 168.

gling individual has not been keenly realized. This is not necessarily to imply that we have had no dramatists capable of recognizing this but it is to state that too frequently these dramatists have been voicing the clichés of their generation. The consequence of this preoccupation is seen in the long-drawn-out animal suffering of contemporary protagonists, and with serious plays that turn on ideologies.

THE KEY TO MORALITY: SPECULATION

Shakespeare, like Sophocles and Euripides before him, found in the ethical values of his era the matter with which he was to concern himself. The great tragedians took their inherited ethical values as a working basis: but only as a working basis. The search for morality was the tragedian's concern. Each move was a struggle of the courageous individual, the prototype of his race,

. . . a man of Greece who dared
To raise in opposition mortal eyes. . . .
[H]e yearned to be the first to break
The bars that hard and fast bound nature's gates.
And thus the vivid vigor of his mind

Prevailed, and he advanced afar beyond
The blazing battlements that walled the world,
And traversed through the limitless universe
By force of reason and of intellect.[6]

Or, to hear Sophocles,

> Man's highest blessedness
> In wisdom chiefly stands.

Man's problem was to search for wisdom in matters

> . . . that touch upon the Gods.

The Greek tragedian was concerned with the "miscarriage of reason." "He was grappling with tremendous problems, he was struggling for a foothold on the brink of unreason, he was confronting the irresponsible demonic forces of creation, he was wrestling for the secrets of destiny; and the groundwork of his tragedy was vast, portentous, and preternatural." [7] In the tragic hero the audiences of Athens saw a man who was aware, even as they, choosing a road of action. His weak-

[6] *De Rerum Natura*, trans. Adelaide, "Conning Tower."
[7] P. H. Frye, *The Theory of Greek Tragedy*, 27.

nesses could be theirs. That he faced imponderables added to the wonder and fascination of it. *Antigone* has become a permanent philosophical problem in that it seems to catch most clearly the Greek mind intent on probing into the nature of evil and morality.

Creon, not Antigone, we may believe, is the tragic hero of *Antigone*. Creon grows, is pulled forward and back; Antigone's character is static. If either character is articulated with the impulses of nature it is Antigone, not Creon, who is neither "unintelligent nor irresponsible." Antigone *feels* her way. The Chorus comments on her,

> She knows not yet
> To yield to evils.

Brought face to face with Creon, face to face that is with a "reasonable" man, she drops her defenses one by one. At the moment of her death she "doubts her own impulse." Reason makes her question natural impulses. Even Creon, rational though he is, is brought low through a native stubbornness. His mind tells him to heed the advice of the seer, Teiresias. Yet he delays until tragedy strikes. There is a moral law, and the man who is self-contained, strong in restraint will come closest to fathoming it. Wise as Oedipus was, he lacked care, consideration in action. Ringed in mystery, he should have taken to thought more readily; he should have curbed the impulses that were instrumental in felling him.

The *dramatis personae* of Sophocles are souls with human dignity, grandeur—and weakness. Ajax, Creon, Oedipus, Odysseus are not static, personified examples of immoral actions, they are questioning human beings. Their misfortune is to have left their minds unguarded "at the point at which circumstance assails it."

We see in examining Greek drama that the tragic hero faced no simple problem when obliged to choose the moral path. Each tragic individual had a weakness to be sure; also, he had a problem that was not easy of solution. His fall originated as much in his failure to comprehend his moral responsibility as in his personal defects of character. The Greek tragedian had no body of Christian morals as his guide. If he had had such moral direction a considerable part of the audience's sympathy with him would have been precluded. If the problem of Shakespeare's tragic heroes resided chiefly or solely in an easy adherence to the Christian ethic Shakespeare's original audience would have had no ambiguous and double emotions to reconcile. Renaissance man discovered that the will to do good was not so simple as some medieval churchmen had envisioned it. There were too many variables. The Renaissance saw, as any intellectually-minded age would have seen, the protagonist hemmed by preternatural forces, the victim of his own blood stream (we have chosen to say glands), of circumstance, and of coincidence. All the instruments of fate are drawn upon by the tragedian—but the essential theme remains: the fall of man is through a failure of his reason. The rational individual in conflict with himself was to the Elizabethan, as to Sophocles and Euripides, the principal glory of the play.

The rational soul was man's ally against nature, the passions in man. In fact the rationale of scholastic philosophy offered a pat explanation, almost a pictorial lesson for the man who would understand his own nature: the will and understanding were the central aspects of the rational soul, as the passions were of the sensible soul. The desires of the passions were judged by the reason, and then the will decided the proper action or denial of action.

If, of course, man were thus simply constructed,

the choice between good and evil would be an unimportant problem. Fortunately, both for the advance of the mind and for the *genre* of tragedy, Renaissance man became intensely interested in the failure of his reason; quite naturally, he recognized that the passions clouded the rational processes. "Coëffeteau," for example, "points out that if because of bad education, custom, unsound organs, bad inclination of will, etc., sensual appetite is not subjected to reason, if appetite is not subject to understanding, then the passions of the sensitive appetite divert a man from following the laws of reason." [8]

Shakespeare is the voice of the rational man's desire to relate himself to an order he conceives as moral:

Since my dear soul was mistress of her choice
And could of men distinguish, her election
Hath seal'd thee for herself; for thou hast been
As one, in suffering all, that suffers nothing;
A man that Fortune's buffets and rewards
Hast ta'en with equal thanks; and blest are those
Whose blood and judgment are so well commingled
That they are not a pipe for Fortune's finger

[8] L. B. Campbell, *Shakespeare's Tragic Heroes,* 68.

To sound what stop she please. Give me that man
That is not passion's slave, and I will wear him
In my heart's core, ay, in my heart of heart,
As I do thee.

In him the audience rediscovers its realization, always just beneath its collective consciousness, of the clash between reason and things as they are. In witnessing the struggle the audience sees a coherent drama of the incoherences, contradictions and irrational involutions that beset mankind. And the audience thereby renews its faith in the eventual powers of reason.

From viewing Greek and Elizabethan tragedy it becomes apparent that to "keep the integrity of the idea, tragedy, within the human being and the race" the individual must "recover or preserve a belief in his worth and dignity in relation to a universe which he comprehends as moral." A period has been experienced in which the morality of the medieval world has been questioned and finally disbelieved. Galileo's compass has, as O'Hara has stated, helped us discover a "Neutral Nature which needed no placation from, and made no moral demands upon, mankind." Consequently, with the partial overthrow of one body of ethics, contemporary man has used rules of thumb, bits of the old morality, and rules based on social necessity but has failed of the effort until more recently—upon recognition of tremendous and almost inexplicable evils—to attempt to evolve a new morality. Some have preferred to call this move toward a new morality an "exploration of the irrational." Terminology means little: morality is the goal.

The Elizabethan was concerned with an inherited morality, and there was little question as to the rightness of the values. The difficulty was in understanding the passions of man. The twentieth century, generally, holds to what are roughly the same moral values—but the problem of understanding the protagonist, man, has become more complex. We have discovered that man has more potential weaknesses than Prospero could have dreamed of. At first sight of them we became discouraged: they are so many.

Twentieth century psychologists have looked so hard at the materials that composed man, preoccupied themselves so one-sidedly with the actions of genes and chromosomes that a new genie sprang up from Sinbad's bottle—an ironic-minded man-made deity. One hesitates to give him any of the old names: but his function was to remind man that the old values had gone, that grandfather's foibles would be those of grandson, that if one walked not with the Jukes the gods alone could be thanked, that man could not add one cubit to his stature by taking thought. Yet in the efforts of some to prove man's ineptitudes new tools were fashioned that are invaluable in working toward a new morality.

There are those whose thoughts are arrived at through individual speculation and searching, who believe in an approach to peace through comprehension of the universe—morality through reason. George Catlin's review of *After Many A Summer Dies the Swan* indicates a new faith of the twentieth century: "Huxley, speaking by the voice of Propter [the hero] grasps that there is a structure of the nature of things, spiritual as also physical, superbly independent of our lusts and wishes, as unconcerned as Spinoza's God about how we feel about it. But in the comprehension of It lies our peace. There also lies the secret of that serene disinterestedness which is the sole pure well, *una sola sancta,* whence flow, not murders and dictatures and wrath, but equity and social justice. Here is to be heard, by those who are willing, a still voice that searches the conscience." [9] But this has been written quite recently.

THE MORAL FRUITION: SPIRIT

George Santayana has defined spirit as "the moral fruition of physical life." He conceives it a "treacherous notion" to conceive of spirit as "disembodied." Essentially spirit "is a moral stress of varying scope and intensity, full of will and selectiveness, arising in animal bodies, and raising their private vicissitudes into a moral experience. The inner light is indeed requisite for focussing impressions and rendering them mentally present, but it is biologically prior to them, vital and central, a product of combustion, a leaping flame, a fountain and seat of judgment. I therefore call it spirit; not that I think it either a substance or a physical power, or capable of existing by itself, but that it is a personal and moral focus of life, where the perspectives of nature are reversed as in a mirror and attached to the fortunes of the single soul." [10]

Such beliefs put the emphasis on the individual

[9] Quoted by G. R. Coffman, "Tragedy and a Sense of the Tragic," *Sewanee Review*, L (Jan.–Mar., 1942), 34.

[10] *The Realm of Spirit*, viii.

personality—and relate particularly to one's life as an intellect. The phrase modern man, at least in one common connotation, seems foreign, divorced from the phrase spiritual man. Actually, if modern is taken to mean critically aware, the former may be parent to the latter. Such a man does not mouth the clichés, the beliefs of his era. He is religious in the fullest sense: the moral goodness, the suffering, the love of men are his concern. In destroying, or attempting to, parts of the primitive, archaic, communal morality of his time, he may appear an enemy to many of his fellows. He sees further than they do and criticizes wrongs they are unaware of.

Spirit, as seen in tragedy at least, has been more often the achievement of the layman than the achievement of the priest. The reasoning is simple: spirit is host to all ideas, it is understanding and judgment, and in its richest life it has been ripened by breadth of experience—love, and a search for omniscience. It is bound by no changeless system.

The Greek, we are told, did not seek out his priests for guidance. The priest had his functions, but those were religious—and Greek life was concerned only in part with religious services and sacrifices. The pursuit of life was larger than one of its aspects. Even religious beliefs of Greece were not consciously kept static. Paul was not pleased that the Athenians had a statue to an unknown god. Such a people, open to the teachings of any seeker after knowledge, could not be satisfied with a body of dogmas. It was their belief that suffering, speculation, fullness in physical and mental life deepened the spirit.

In the "passing" of Oedipus, as envisioned by Sophocles, one discovers a man who has endured, and who has won his way to calm, to the spirit that is born of understanding. In this province of the moral life the inharmonious heterogeneity of humanly suffered events are resolved. Such scenes appear in Shakespeare and in all pure tragedies. Reason and will in conflict with passion create the tragic hero's dilemma: in his rise to spirit all struggle falls into focus. A sense of calm suffuses his being, and is his reward.

Professor Campbell, as we have indicated, has explained Renaissance tragedy largely in terms of medieval didacticism: "Tragedy teaches negatively . . . and . . . by tragedy 'we are taught by a Collecting of fatal Events, to avoid Ruin and Misery.' "[11] Thus Lear becomes a study of "wrath in

[11] *Shakespeare's Tragic Heroes,* 24.

old age," Othello, of the "tragedy of jealousy," Macbeth "of fear," Hamlet "of grief"; and tragedy becomes an extension of medieval *exempla*. If this, thus simply, were the total wealth of Elizabethan tragedy the speeches of Macbeth and Lear and Hamlet and Othello would be akin to speeches of fallen heroes in the metrical tragedies of Tudor England, speeches bearing witness to the design of God in punishing sin. The tragic hero sees more than is conceived of in orthodox scholastic philosophy. There's more to the puzzle than adherence to Christian ethics:

> Why should a dog, a horse, a rat, have life,
> And thou no breath at all?

is the anguished question of Lear. In witness of Lear's suffering Albany says:

> . . . we that are young
> Shall never see so much, nor live so long.

Ultimately, there is but one thing—

> Ripeness is all.

At death, Brutus has learned his bones

. . . have but labour'd to attain this hour.

There was a morality to be observed—there was an enigma to be wondered at. At the core of tragedy there was an unanswered question, and only the man of judgment and experience could dare ask it. The dogmatic moralist could not; but then, no unquestioning moralist could write tragedy.

The sequence of late Western attitudes toward tragedy, Professor Campbell would have it, is this: from tragic falls man was to discover "by example the sins that must be avoided if the destruction demanded as God's revenge were to be escaped; finally, that he was to learn vicariously the vices and passions that might lead to his own destruction." This interpretation of medieval "tragedy" is undoubtedly tenable: but there was no pure tragedy in medieval Europe. To ignore the spiritual overtones of Elizabethan tragedy is to oversimplify.

The surface of the oppressive collectivism of the medieval faith was broken through, the skies parted, pushed apart by the hands of Kepler and Copernicus. The aware man discovered himself as the new Prometheus, no longer opposed to Zeus but to whatever forces that would destroy him. Only at such a moment could Shakespeare, "freed from theological uses," have uttered "the boundless poem we have within our hearts." Professor E. E. Stoll has written that tragedy since the Renaissance has been prevailingly "pagan." "Christianity, like some philosophy, is an alien system of values, which deprecates the passions, inculcates renunciation, and holds death to be the gate of life. It is too comforting, too dogmatic and unpoetical. God and Heaven in the *finale* would break or dull the tragic point as Zeus and Hades do not." [12] The spiritual elevation that can come only when a hero has learned to find his strength within himself is the keystone of the structure of tragedy.

The philosophical attitudes of the *modern*—not the pseudomodern—man of the twentieth century are little different from those of Euripides or Bruno or Shakespeare. He of all his fellows is at the very edge of the furthest advances man has made. He knows that man has worked painfully up the ladder—and he knows how shaky the ladder is; or, to change the image, he is perfectly aware of the almost infinite complexity of the organized machine—and as perfectly aware that it seems to be shaking apart under stress of its own effort. For every hope, he finds a doubt. He has one basic criterion:

[12] *Shakespeare and Other Masters,* 76.

never to accept the palliatives so dear to the mass of mankind. He will remain an individual personality, for only thus can he, in the freedom of his own experience, reach the understanding that is spirit.

Fortunately, the new temper of the contemporary serious play indicates a search for values that fulfill the spirit. One of a number of such plays is Robert Sherwood's *Abe Lincoln in Illinois.* It may be that the Lincoln myth has a partially false basis, but Lincoln has become a symbol of spiritual strength, as though he were a strong member of the house of Atreus. Sherwood's expressed interest in Lincoln is as a spiritual, *not psychological,* protagonist. And this is the play's significance. Here is a man who wins a spiritual victory. Stifled in an overhanging mist of evil he suffers his way to an understanding of the futility of hiding within himself. Sherwood may not have created a tragic hero, he has created a spiritual hero. There are a number of similar characters in the plays of Maxwell Anderson. That this recent step is upward and most significant is to be inferred from a now dated comment of O'Neill's in regard to the Hairy Ape. "[He] was a symbol of man who has lost his old harmony with nature, the harmony which he used to have as an animal and has not yet acquired in a spiritual way." O'Neill's theatre was concerned with an intervening strata, the psychological. Fortunately the recent theatre has striven to rise to the spiritual level.

As a recent novelist states it, this attitude is that for which America is groping: "What man wanted was simplicity affirmed and informed and made wise and workable by tragic experience. . . . That was what America wanted for the assuagement of his [the central character's] nostalgia, his loneliness, his sense of loss. He wanted the laying of a ghost of broken promises that had so long haunted him and the coming true of dreams that would trouble him until fulfilled." [13] Few artists have managed to attain the vision: little wonder that contemporary letters pathetically speak of those who walk only on the periphery of things, those unaware that they have

> . . . that within that passeth show.

[13] Struthers Burt, *Along These Streets.*

Tragic Failures

ROMANTICISM

SHAKESPEAREAN tragedy augured, in its romantic qualities, the decadence of Elizabethan dramatic tragedy. The suggestion of the impersonal, of ultimate repose and dignity, and of decorum is antithetical to the always uneasy romantic mind. Classical tragedy is a clarified art, above the restlessness and indecision of romantic art. In the *Bacchae* there is such a romantic spirit, but the romantic tendency did not strongly affect the Greek tragedians. Perhaps the longer life of Greek tragedy was due in part to the relative exclusion of the adventures, the dynamic actions and characters that were used by Shakespeare. In fact it was not until the twilight of Greece that such romances as *Daphnis and Chloe* were written. Stories of shipwrecks, of enchanted isles, of long lost brothers and sisters are inspired by a different spirit than that which gave Greek tragedy its soul. Such themes appealed to the aging Shakespeare and to Beaumont and Fletcher, and to Massinger. Tragedy could not long survive this atmosphere.

The romanticism of Shakespeare—the "panoramic" structure, the mass of individuals, the confusion of action, the seeming lack of motives—does not rest in itself. He manages a tragic synthesis as a basis for his "music of the hidden spirit . . . [and his expression] of the inchoate movements of man's unuttered dreams." He offers no definitive beliefs—other than that man should possess himself in reason—for moral conduct; but he does supply a warning: in a world of "improvident possibilities" one's "readiness is all." A Sophoclean core is seen in the romantic amalgam; romantic indecisiveness is given focus in a profound philosophical realization.

Perhaps the "temptation" to inchoate romantic fluxions occurs most forcefully when confusion begins to overtake the believers in a moral order. Certainly it has less place in Aeschylus and Sophocles and more in Euripides, who was inclined to see more variables in the Pattern; and for Shakespeare, coming as the medieval stream backed into innumerable tributaries, there was little possibility of a strongly classical view, even if that had been most desirable. Unfortunately Shakespeare had no late contemporaries writing plays who were able to keep even his balance. Elizabethan earnestness in *Romeo and Juliet* becomes Cavalier sentimentality in *A King and No King;* the romantic virus works a while longer and *Valentinian* is written. When tragedy threatens to cease being an exposition of man's search for a moral order then dramas that in themselves merely entertain and delight are substituted. "The fiber of life is weakening when such fashion prevails." The pallor of melancholy, the posings of courtly love, the tragi-comic realm is being substituted for the rigors of tragedy. A similar transformation had occurred in the tragedy written and inspired by Euripides. "[T]he deformation of his tragedy as a *genre* was evidently in the direction of late or modern comedy." [1]

Romanticism is, of course, concerned with the tremendous worth of the individual—but not only with the individual. One type of romantic mind is never satisfied with generic qualities; it must push on to the point where the individual is

[1] P. H. Frye in his *Romance and Tragedy* gives a very full treatment to this entire theme.

unique—and therefore, usually, exaggerated. At that point where the individual ceases to mirror the universal in man the protagonist ceases to have significance as a tragic figure. Obviously, the classical spirit can universalize to the point where the individual is only a ghastly reflection of the shadow of a man. It would seem, however, that the former failure is the more frequent. The resemblances among men—as long as the tragic view is being striven for—are far more important than the differences. Shades of character are vital in the creation of a protagonist to the extent that he is representative as well as unique.

Exaggeration in the direction of universal goodness personified in the tragic hero seems to have been less germane to the Renaissance mind than exaggerated evil. At least wilful villains are more common to the area bordering on tragedy. The very wilfulness of such protagonists precludes satisfying vicarious experience for the auditor. The audience must see its idealized self on the stage as well as its concurrently blind or evil self. Such villains may be the "heroes" of serious drama; they are never tragic heroes. The Medea of Seneca is such a figure. Tamburlaine—a Superman in anticipation of Nietzsche—Selimus, and

Barabas are others. Such exaggerated figures are indigenous in English drama, but they swaggered their romantic way particularly across the boards of the Restoration theatre. Their story has been told by Bonamy Dobrée, who emphasizes that the failure of this genre was in the attempts of dramatists to "express romantic ideas in a form especially evolved for the classical."

The greatest weakness—the desire for the regions beyond tragedy—inherent in the romantic quest is discovered at the point where the romantic mind turns mystic. The poet discovers a realm, mysterious and preternatural and emotionally satisfying (although enervating) beyond which he finds it hard to go. It is the world of Tristram and Isolt, mournful, shadowy—unreal. In this realm of shadow man is lost, he hears only the wailing cry of a frightened animal, the whimpering of a pathetic creature who has lost her way. It is the world of Maurice Maeterlinck's *Pelleas and Melisande* and *The Blind*, fantasies not tragedies. The atmosphere is the thing, a world that never was is bodied forth for its brief hour—signifying nothing. In the area of tragedy there is strife, effort, a refusal to bow before the yoke—in this area of romance there is only brooding contemplation. Yeats failed, for one reason, in his early plays to restore tragedy to our theatre for this same reason, a love of the misty isles. Spirit grows out of struggle; it is not found in the hopeful visions of those who find no strong sanctuary within themselves. As much as any single reason perhaps, their succumbing to mysticism has kept some romantic poets from the creation of tragedy. The pale blue light of the mystic vision is death to tragedy.

To go on, to attempt more minute definitions of the highly elusive attitudes, and illustrations thereof, that we generally have labelled romantic, is unnecessary, because contemporary writers are not particularly inclined toward romanticism. The chief romantic heresy of the contemporary theatre is easily recognizable.

In "Yes, by the Eternal,"[2] Maxwell Anderson seems to be restating the general beliefs of Dryden. Anderson writes: ". . . the authors of tragedy offer the largest hope for mankind which I can discern in the great poetry of the earth, a hope that man is greater than his clay, that the spirit of man may rise superior to physical defeat and death. . . . The message of tragedy is simply

[2] An essay in *Essence of Tragedy.*

that men are better than they think they are, and this message needs to be said over and over again in every tongue lest the race lose faith in itself entirely."

Here the errors of Dryden are repeated. The poetry of tragedy does most certainly have glorifications of man as a basis. But this is not all. Authors of Restoration tragedies set out to glorify man—and how ridiculous they become; more so than certain of our commercial playwrights, as we shall see, who are concerned with destroying the moulds in which modern naturalism has flourished.

SUPERNATURALISM

Our humanistic heritage makes it impossible for certain contemporaries to look upon plays shot through with supernaturalism as *tragic;* or, to put it more specifically, plays in which supernaturalism dictates the action.[3]

[3] A related theme is the chthonic myth. In one sense, the *Oresteia* of Aeschylus has become an historical document. Perhaps the audience of Aeschylus was closer to, and could accept more readily, a communal morality, the blood-tie, and the obligation of vengeance. The chthonic myth is central in Aeschylus' treatment of Orestes. In the struggle of the protagonist the Athenian audience saw the civilized mind wrench responsibility from the family and give it to the state. To most of us who are concerned more with individual men than with morality in

"The profane poet," Santayana writes in an early essay, "is by instinct a naturalist. He loves landscape, he loves love, he loves the humor and pathos of earthly existence." He is of this earth —and willingly. The religious poet frequently loves none of these things—and therefore posits values he cannot find in his natural self; he creates those things, in an autonomous part of his being; he needs to supplement the insufficiencies of the natural order. The profane and the religious poet speak for two different worlds. The tragic experi-

the cosmic design this concern of Aeschylus with the chthonic myth and its being worked out until cosmic harmony is restored is distant and almost irrelevant. It is drama we can imaginatively accept as fable or ancient myth, but which needs a humanistic emphasis to make it pertinent for us. See Philip Wheelwright, "Poetry, Myth and Reality," *The Language of Poetry*, 24–25.

Family Reunion, among its many complexities, appears to be repetitious of the Aeschylean theme of an inherited obligation of retribution. To be sure, there is such a mixture of naturalistic, Christian and Greek tradition in the play that a simple statement is impossible. At least a part of Harry's working out of the curse he has been born under is his indirect murder of his mother, first in the actual (?) killing of his wife, a woman whose tentacles choked him as surely as those of his mother, and secondly in his leaving which immediately kills his mother. Both he and Agatha know what his going will do to Amy, his mother. *Family Reunion* is the *Oresteia* over again. All the actions of Harry are in expiation of a curse, slow and unalterable in its working out. Harry must suffer his way through to redemption for the sins of his parents. He does not bathe his hands in his mother's blood but he is consciously the instrument of her punishment. The theory of *Family Reunion* would seem to fail then on at least this score, Harry willingly undertakes the ancient obligation of blood vengeance.

ence belongs to the world of the profane poet—even though the poet may, in the part of his being that feels obliged to posit "religious truths," accept nontragic values. The tragedian, whose first concern is the mind and then the spirit of the tragic protagonist cannot bring in the irrelevancies of autonomous beliefs and maintain a primary interest in matters of the earth. The protagonist is doing battle with his natural self, his passions and the natural world about him. The tragic experience moves toward a definite finale—it sticks close to the observable facts of life. It is beyond revelation. To oversimplify, tragedy may be thought of as the integrating moral force in the secular realm that faith is in the religious realm. The contemporary reader can see this most readily in Shakespeare, and, accepting his tragedy as a norm, can note certain supernatural elements in other plays that seem to lessen or even to destroy their effectiveness as tragedy.

The Shakespearean tone is a blend of "natural superstition, conventional reverence, egotistical emotion [and] complete agnosticism." According to the plausible interpretation of Dr. Wile, Hamlet was not only a remarkable student and scholar, he likewise was a deeply religious man. Against this religious feeling there was his philosophy of skepticism. Therein lies the tragedy of the character. Thus there is no doubt certainly that ghosts and witches are actual participants in the Shakespearean scene, not hallucinations. The witches, for example, are necessary compromises with contemporary superstition, and are valuable dramatic symbols. In *Macbeth* the witches are personifications of destinal forces who despite the part they play in motivating the actions of Macbeth do not geld him of his will and personal responsibility. Macbeth has no latent impulsion to do certain things, either under the impulse of God or the Three Sisters: the choice is his. Thus the presence of preternatural beings can hardly be said to preclude tragic treatment.

In the *Oresteia* the Furies are "really the protagonists of the trilogy." [4] That Orestes is dismissed rather peremptorily, that the concern of the dramatist is with reconciling the Furies with the new order of things are the disturbing factors for the contemporary reader. Aeschylus' concern is with

[4] See, for a full discussion of this problem, C. E. Whitmore, *The Supernatural in Tragedy*. Also, it should be added, the German literary critic Father Otto Meller in his studies of tragedy has emphasized that Christian doctrines are foreign values to the realm of tragedy. His conclusions are, I believe, substantially in agreement with mine.

a preternatural world, which is related to the human world to be sure but which in its majesty overshadows man's problems. Aeschylus is first a theologian, a man who posits the dogmas he believes in. He is too far from our more vital, central problem of human passion. In Sophocles the gods are present, but they are behind the scenes and the dominant interest. Briefly: "Aeschylus is interested in the supernatural primarily because it reveals to him the springs of human action; Sophocles regards it as one more thread to be woven harmoniously into his design." In *Euripides the Rationalist*, a study by Dr. A. W. Verrall, the appearances of the gods is held a "mere theatrical trick" by the last of the great Greek tragedians. At least Euripides does not respect the gods, and does handle them mechanically. They are not a "real constituent of [his] dramatic fabric." In comparing his work with Elizabethan tragedy and contemporary approaches to tragedy the common attitude found in all makes Euripides seem quite modern in tone. Certainly there is nothing like complete faith in Euripides: of this much we can be certain. The presence of supernatural creatures in a tragedy is not the thing: the part they play is. In Aeschylus we feel that supernatural powers may intervene at any moment, in Sophocles and in Euripides usually we do not.

In such plays, however, as the *Hippolytos,* wherein the *deus ex machina* appearance of Artemis is used to effect a change in the action, and in *Heracles,* wherein Lyssa (Madness) takes a decisive part, the modern reader sees a "dramatic solecism." Those critics who demand preoccupation with actual supernatural figures actively concerned with human endeavor are quite right in seeing the development of decadence in Sophocles and Euripides. We can see in this cycle of Greek drama that the tragedy—as it can be accepted in the twentieth century at least—is religion remembered, but the moral basis of which is accepted not as an absolute guide but only as a tentative yardstick against which the partially agnostic tragedian attempts his own measurements. When man's destiny is thus arbitrarily changed by an intervening supernatural power, man's strength is not seen to rest in himself. English drama since Shakespeare has seen such belief in the arbitrary intervention by the Deity, or, at the least, has seen strong supernatural suasion brought to bear against the protagonist.

From at least the time of Boethius this potential suasion has in literature been found in a personal God, benevolent, omniscient, and directive. Under such a deity—be there temporal chaos or temporal order—the ultimate waited "in the hands of God." Consequently despite what the appearance may have been to a limited human vision all fortune was good. When this doctrine was allowed in explicit statement on the stage it meant death to tragedy.

Even in periods subsequent to Shakespeare this same metaphysic has for the general precluded tragedy. One can turn to a seventeenth and to a twentieth century example.

No doubt it is true that the faith of Milton, even as of Dante, gives a certain "sublimity" to his work. That is Milton's strength. Milton, however, as Professor H. C. Grierson points out, is concerned with "the thought of God as directly inspiring men by latent impulsion to do certain things. . . ." Samson is "under the inspiration of God." [5]

There are irremediable evils in the world against which man must contend—without avail. Man's victories will be only of the spirit, in his refusal

[5] *Milton and Wordsworth,* 139.

to cringe or to give up in the face of evil and the inexplicable whims of chance. To Milton, as to Samson, there is in the long view nothing inexplicable: there is a pattern of action designed by an omniscient and just providence. Says the Chorus at the end of the poem:

> All is best, though we often doubt
> What the unsearchable dispose
> Of highest wisdom brings about,
> And ever best found in the close.

Samson accepts the ills he suffered as a just punishment:

> Nothing of all these evils hath befallen me
> But justly.

The hero is an instrument, not a victim, of Providence. He may question the means of expressing but not the *end* of God's design:

> Why was my breeding ordered and prescribed
> As a person separate to God,
> Designed for great exploits; if I must die
> Betrayed, captived, and both my eyes put out
> Made of my enemies the scorn of Gaza.

. . . .

But peace, I must not quarrel with the will
Of highest dispensation, which herein
Haply hath ends beyond my reach to know.

Milton, also, of course, was writing as an orthodox believer. Death would not come as a conqueror to Samson, it would come to release him:

This one prayer yet remains, might I be heard,
No long petition, speedy death
The close of all my miseries and the balm.

Curiously similar in tone and content is Eliot's *Murder in the Cathedral.* If the poet's intention was to write a tragedy he chose an unfortunate theme, at once akin to a medieval mystery and a medieval tragedy. The tone and philosophical pattern is Christian and medieval.

And I am not in danger: only near death,

says Becket. He is willing to die a martyr. He has tried all these:

Delight in sense, in learning and in thought,
Music and philosophy, curiosity,
The purple bullfinch in the lilac tree,
The tiltyard skill, the strategy of chess,—

and found they were not enough. The four tempters, allegorical characters from the world of Chaucer and Lydgate, are put behind him. Indeed, the very wheel of the goddess Fortuna is borne witness to:

> The fool, fixed in his folly only may think
> He can turn the wheel on which he turns.

The two concepts—personal rejection of sin and acceptance of rigorous fortune—may seem mutually exclusive. Actually they are coexistent. Yet Becket had no choice, really. "Destiny," the Chorus tells us,

> . . . waits in the hand of God, shaping the still unshapen:
> I have seen these things in a shaft of sunlight.
> Destiny waits in the hand of God, not in the hands of statesmen
> Who do, some well, some ill, planning and guessing,
> Having their aims which turn in their hands in the pattern of time.

Fortuna holds the final decision. Eliot has written a dramatic poem, a metrical drama, but not a dramatic tragedy. His philosophical pattern is in relation to tragedy "ignoble": like Samson, Thomas à Becket finds his strength not in himself but in God.

The importance of Eliot and his work tends to make supernaturalism appear an important contemporary theme. Actually our theatre has been little influenced by romanticism or by supernaturalism. Naturalism, on the other hand, has been her philosophical and structural basis.

NATURALISM

In every great age there seems to have been a cycle, a decline from nobility to naturalism. In the work of some artists, such as Verrocchio, we see ourselves in the forms that express nobility. Again, the "pressure of reality" may become so intense that the mien of nobility seems false, and we see only the "reality" minus the nobility. One man, one age will see nobility as an aspect of the total reality, another man and another age as only a recollected state of mind imagined by dewy-eyed forebears. Those who find it difficult, considering our inheritance, to accept nobility should consider this: Nobility "is not an artifice that the mind has added to human nature. The mind has added nothing to human nature. It [nobility] is a violence from within that protects from a violence without. It is imagination pressing back against the pressure of reality." [6] The dramatist whose mind patterns are founded in naturalism or realism neglects to "press back against reality." Obviously the tragic vision—the soul of which is nobility—is hard to sustain. Though nobility is latent in every age the "pressure of reality" is at times so intense that the spirit of nobility seems nowhere to be found. The matter of naturalistic drama is seen everywhere about us. The composition of tragedy must come largely from within. Further, those subjects that border on the abnormal have the interest of the sensational.

Although Euripides has the usual inclinations of the confirmed intellectual toward studies in the abnormalities of character, he does not seem to have been much concerned with neurotic brutality. Perhaps intellectualism had not had time enough by his day to turn inward upon itself to the point where masochism may become a desired end. There is however a direct connection between neuroticism in Elizabethan drama and in contem-

[6] Wallace Stevens, "The Noble Rider," *The Language of Poetry*, 91–125.

porary literature. *The Duchess of Malfi,* composed equally of sugary sentiments and neurotic brutality, appeals to those morbidly interested in disillusionment and pessimism. Strangled women and children, choral singing and hysterical observations by madmen—the perversion of using horror for its own sake. Morbidity of character again becomes its own value, related only to masochism, in Ford's *The Broken Heart*. Characters ebb away into nothingness—sometimes with no apparent cause. Orgilus bleeds slowly to death after cutting his own veins, Penthea and Calantha die of grief. All is melancholy and sorrow. Yet no one is quite fully aware of the *whys* of so much suffering, other than that the characters are strangely obsessed with a sentimental melancholy. They are in a world that knows suffering as its chief "value." It is a type of literature that, as T. R. Short has observed, is akin to the "most powerful literature of our own day, . . . a vein in life which Shakespeare, in *Troilus and Cressida,* and a few later playwrights worked." The abnormality of searching out suffering because "pleasure is too little," as Robinson Jeffers does, is not to grant man dignity but perversion. Jeffers may use the figures of Ajax, Orestes, Oedipus, but his are not tragic figures—sexual abnormality, insanity and masochistic tortures may belong to the literary milieu of Erskine Caldwell and William Faulkner, they have nothing to do with the tragic vision. Madrone Bothwell, a character in Jeffers' senseless pageant of pain, whispers,

These friendly burrs my
Comforters: I am afraid I have hurt them a little,
I have rolled in them.

The burrs that Lear suffered were not of the flesh; he did not think of them as friendly. Edgar in an aside to the audience warned against just that:

> Bad is the trade that must play fool to sorrow.

There are irrational monsters in Euripides quite as divorced from tragedy as monsters in Elizabethan and contemporary drama. The Electra of Euripides, the Alice of *Arden of Feversham,* the Lavinia of *Mourning Becomes Electra* are alike in at least this respect: each is pathologically abnormal, and therefore lacking in the quality of universality necessary for tragedy. Whereas the Electra of Sophocles is a complex personality strong and admirable in all but one aspect of her character, the Electra of Euripides is a vindictive, middle-aged harpy, "implacable, self-centered, fantastic in hatred, callous to the verge of insanity." A horde of such vicious, totally misguided women as Alice of *Arden of Feversham* appear in the bloody melodramas of Elizabeth's era. Their like was sung of in ballads and marvelled at in chapbooks. Their pathological unbalance was the secret of their capacity for stirring interest—somewhat in the way that readers marvelled at hearing of the birth of two-headed children. Alice says to her husband:

What, groan'st thou? Nay, then, give me the weapon!
Take this for hindering Mosbie's love and mine.

The capacity for melodramatic action inherent in the neurotic Lavinia Mannon of *Mourning Becomes Electra* rounds out the series. Lavinia is a dramatization of a typical case study out of contemporary psychology. She holds our interest as a pathological type, lost in the mazes of a mind she is incapable of fathoming—an invitation to naturalistic treatment.

If the naturalistic dramatist is willing to recognize the presence of frustration, conflict, and disorder in the universe—and no one will gainsay him—then he should be willing to look for the presence of "order, structure, system, form and pattern in the universe." Perhaps we can never understand fully, at least we can increase our penetration. It may be that life is nothing but effort, but certainly a static society is neither possible nor desirable. The naturalistic dramatist, in a sense, presents a static view—is concerned only with conflict, disorder and frustration. The tragic view enables one to approach an understanding of the most daring speculations into moral philosophy. Speculation is necessary if any intellectual advances are to be made, for only thereby can any new perspectives be attained. "In the absence of perspective"—we have A. N. Whitehead's word for it—"there is triviality." Although it may be unfair to the authors of naturalistic literature to label their work trivial it does not seem unfair to take note of their limited view.

Again, some proclivity in the artist too often spurs him to hobgoblin consistency in viewpoint. The great spirit—the Shakespeare—can crush the flower for its perfume and quietly witness the bursting of the mighty heart. In the majestic, the great, the commonplace, the drab, the distasteful, the agonizing the spirit can find its tragic, lyric, or prosaic release. Each facet of the drama begs for consideration. The truly tragic is but one response—albeit the highest—of the spirit to the scenes on the revolving stage. The areas of experience bordering on the tragic are not to be despised because they too are not tragic; they, for balanced chiaroscuro of the spirit, must be accepted; without them the exaltation of the tragic could not be felt.

If the grandeur of an unconquered succumbing quickly and finally to death is not necessarily a life situation, the dramatist should not therefore deny his protagonist the fulfillment of his death. When the formlessness of living, the surface of the ambient moods of a thousand secret impulses, is allowed on the stage the function of the tragedian is precluded. The poet, as Aristotle insisted, is not an historian; the poet is concerned with what might happen—"for poetry tends rather to express what is universal." Death in tragedy most certainly is a dramatic device, but a necessary device. In front of the curtain of death the values of the individual, of fame, of human enjoyments are most sharply outlined. For the dramatist to refuse death its part in the tragedy is to preclude the most significant scenes in tragedy. Or perhaps this is to overstate. Certainly the Oedipus of *Oedipus Tyrannus* is greater in his ruin than is Jocasta, who is "blotted out." Yet the Greek tragedians generally recognized the need for the finality of death in the construction of their dramas. So, too, all but invariably, did the Elizabethans. Not so, however, contemporary dramatists. In both versions of *Ethan Frome* the protagonist is denied any release. For Ethan, and for Mattie and Zeena, there is only frustration, drawn-out and unmitigated. Ethan has only the dignity of his quiet endurance.

The critic, often subversive, negative, embittered, is a boon to his society but is rarely a poet, and almost never a tragic poet. Or to state the problem more explicitly the tragedian must be a critic, and a keen one, of the world he sees and feels about him. But his tragic vision must come to the fore to elevate and ennoble his reaction, however bitter, as a critic. He must, as Shakespeare did, move from *Timon of Athens* to *Hamlet*. Even when the critic who is also a poet does appear the "pressure of reality" may so crush his heart that he will flail back at the irrationalities —and lose the calm that must ultimately be breathed into the spirit of the tragic protagonist. Some episodes in the human story are too depressing for tears, and offer, considering the limitations of the world that still is, no possibility of reconciling ethics and morality. These problems may be legitimate concerns of naturalistic, psychological or sociological drama but not of tragic drama. The critical concern may be with certain stupidities in orthodox churches, with the viciousness of war, with the nearsighted practices demanded by social mores—but unless the auditor may rise above pity in witnessing a protagonist at odds with these "dislocations" in the universe there will be no tragic experience.

If one considers *The Trojan Women* as an attack on the injustice and blood-lust of the Greeks in slaughtering their Trojan enemy it becomes a comment on wilful cruelty. It is a protest against society, against the injustices done to the Trojan women,

> . . . far-flung to slavery and the bread
> Of shame in Hellas, over bitter seas.

These are wrongs reparable by learning to love peace and to respect the sanctity of foreign hearths. There is no tragic conflict here, no character caught in interstices of a tragic net, at least partly of his own weaving. There is no self-deception in the Trojan women: they are the victims of an unreasonable human order. This is man against man, not man against Fate. *Timon of Athens* gives promise of being a tragedy, but falls short of what may have been the dramatist's aim and succeeds if at all only as a satire. A common theme—misplaced generosity—may underlie both *Lear* and *Timon;* one is a tragedy, the other a satire. The inability of certain contemporary poets to see a core of order in the universe results in such moving—and depressing—works as Auden and Isherwood's *The Ascent of F-6.* Michael Ransom, the protagonist, would attempt to conquer himself, would search for a meaning if only he knew where to look. Ransom's motives for attempting to scale F-6 are unknown to himself: the causes of human failure and action are too complex, and man munches comfortably on the old chestnuts. Here, at least, there is a search for a problem, the prerequisite to searching for a moral core. But the dramatists offer no hope:

> . . . the great ordered flower itself is
> withering. . . .

Psychology—which too easily becomes the rationalization for materialism—is basic to all tragedy, to all analyses of character, Greek, Elizabethan, or contemporary. When the tragedian stops at the level of psychology, he may be stimulating emotionally or intellectually, he may write in the manners we have come to know as naturalism and realism—he will not write tragedy. Analysis has limitations inherent in its own nature. Spirit is essential to the tragic vision, and although beyond analysis, it is not averse to analysis. Spirit recognizes nature, her potentialities and effects; it allows that, above nature, there is wisdom in foresight, hindsight, contradictions and comparisons. But when thought works to defeat itself, when it becomes so obsessed with the intricacies and mazes of its own being, hypnotized by the whirling kaleidoscope of its own ideas confusion mothers despair. Spirit "in its virtual omniscience" can envelop confusion and rise above despair. Spiritual experience, "as it grows clearer, seems to widen the gulf between the victim and his predicaments; until the innate claims and dignity of the spirit assert themselves as rights, against an even infinite pressure of facts and circumstances." [7] Dramatists, even potential tragedians, who become permanently depressed by the "pressure of reality" cut themselves off from the tragic creation.

[7] Santayana, *The Realm of Spirit,* 119–181.

The Poetic Diction of Tragedy

I

POETRY is to the tragedian what light is to the stage designer. Robert Edmond Jones speaks of the "livingness of light." "Lucidity, penetration, awareness, discovery, inwardness, wonder. . . . These are the qualities we should try to achieve in our lighting," he says.[1] Atavisms from out of the womb of the world, a sense of evil darkness, shadows stealing over a sunlit scene, potential horrors slowly rising from the unmeasured depths of man's mind—these are the poet's concern.

Suffering is the common denominator of the tragic experience: it makes possible nobility of character; it gives significance to evil, both inherent in the world and man-made; it gives meaning to the fact of death. But without poetic language intense to the point of making the auditor

[1] *The Dramatic Imagination,* 121.

experience suffering vicariously the dramatic portrayal of suffering makes only for pathos, or disgust. A Wagnerian theme without music would be a primitive horror, a nightmare of bestial cruelty. The rhythms soothe us, lessen the terror —and finally transmute pain into joy. Eloquence, poetry, is one of the keys to the paradox of a tragedian's portrayal of suffering that exalts us and gives us pleasure; only thus expressed can suffering be changed into a distillate of exquisite joy. Somehow the auditor knows, senses, that an indefinable beauty is on the underside of the medal of suffering:

> With what beseechings, through what agonies
> Beauty besought first dwelt in this dark clay;
> How delicately that blossom of the skies
> Was nursed, that no lone petal might decay:
> Oh, by what ardors! by what sacrifice! [2]

Only through poetic images are we able to express such feelings with any satisfactory adequacy, for as Santayana says in "Tragic Philosophy": "We cannot express a feeling more sincerely than by rehearsing all the images, all the metaphors,

[2] A.E., *Vale and Other Poems,* 47.

which it suggests to us. . . . Dramatic poetry is an excursus in this direction; it reports the echoes which events produce in a voluminous inner sensibility; it throws back our perception of what is going on into the latent dream which this perception has for its background. . . . These natural harlequins, the passions, are perfectly sincere in their falsehoods and indirections: their fancy is their only means of expressing the facts."

Santayana continues with a discussion of the moral censor, the "inner man" whose "function is to forbid the utterance, in the council chamber within us, of unparliamentary sentiments, and to suppress all reports not in the interest of our moral dignity." Thus if the censor "had got at Juliet in time" she would not have imagined Romeo cut up into little stars—every atom of him being passionately loved by her—rather, she "would have said, 'What is Romeo's body to me? Our spirits will be reunited in heaven!' This would have been a sham. . . ." This censor bobs up frequently—but he has many opponents, and is therefore not dangerous. But he has an ostrich-headed cousin who is only slightly less harmful to dramatic poetry. A false desire to shut out the unpleasant and ugly causes this cousin to exclude from consideration all objects which, as Addison puts it, are not "Great, Surprising, or Beautiful."

Two distinct vistas, then, loom before the eyes of the inquirer into dramatic tragedy. There is a beauty that is the result of careful selection, the primrose minus the thorns, the blue sky and fleecy clouds minus suggestions of jagged lightning and raucous thunder. The other vista holds the heterogeneous complexities of the everyday scene. Here one can see the toad sitting on the edge of a marsh sunning itself, or hear the screech of the hoot owl on a clear night, or witness the funeral on a pleasant morning of the man who has died from cancer. The former is romantic and a conscious reordering by the poet of the world he sees about him, the latter—for want of a better term—is metaphysical and represents a refusal on the part of the poet to exclude experiences from his consciousness simply because they are unlovely. There is no absolute way of separating the two kinds of poetry.

In dramatic tragedy both types of poetry must exist, poetry of exclusion (emotional) and poetry of synthesis (intellectual). Let us borrow a thought from Socrates, as reported by a contemporary of ours: " 'Poetry,' maintains Socrates, 'feeds and waters the passions instead of drying them up: she lets them rule instead of ruling them, as they ought to be ruled, with a view to the happiness and virtue of mankind.' 'I cannot deny it,' replies Glaucon, and the conclusion is that, when the honey-gathering Muses are at work, pleasure and pain will rule in the state and not reason." Plato is asking for the light of reason, the examination and reflection upon many facts. Plutarch was wiser, for in commending music, he wrote that "the soul was 'not altogether amenable to precept and instruction, and redeemable from vice only by reason, but that it needed some other persuasion, a moulding and softening influence to co-operate with reason.' "[3] It may be submitted that the metaphysical elements of the poetry of dramatic tragedy lessen the danger of emotional debauchery on the part of the auditor. Ironic poetry is intellectual, as is the introspective poetry uttered by many tragic heroes; and so, too, is a preventative of emotional debauchery. On the other hand, we feel pity, sympathy, compassion, and to refuse to utter our feelings about them is to deny human experience. But to see only these things is to oversimplify. Before dramatic tragedy can be a valid representation it must reflect the

[3] W. M. Dixon, *Tragedy*, 123–124.

total tragic experience. Both types of poetry must therefore obtain in the pure dramatic tragedy. The spirit of beauty in suffering is wedded to the spirit of inquiry; their child is tragedy.

II

The language of the poet, said Aristotle, "must be clear and it must not be mean." To use only current words was to be mean, to use strange words was to be obscure. The answer, so far as poetry in tragedy is concerned, he wrote, was a metaphorical diction, used in iambic verse. "For this is the metre closest to the prose of ordinary life, as befits an imitation of that life; and a poetic diction which is mainly metaphorical can keep closest to the vocabulary of ordinary life also. 'The gift for metaphor,' adds Aristotle, 'is the greatest of all. This alone cannot be taught, but is a mark of natural genius; for it implies an inborn eye for likenesses.' "[4] Yet, as Professor Gilbert Murray implies, the metaphors of Greek tragedy are not tumbled together in profusion as are the metaphors of, say, Shakespeare. English is an "ornate" language, Greek an "austere" one, and "a direct translation produce[s] an effect of

[4] E. V. Lucas, *Tragedy*, 125.

baldness which [is] quite unlike the original." But this is a difference of degree, not of kind. A translation of a romantic passage from Aeschylus appeals to us no doubt as fully as it did to his original audience.

> Black smoke I would be
> nearing the clouds of God.
> All unseen, soaring aloft,
> as dust without wings I would perish.
> Oh, for a seat high in air,
> Where the dripping cliffs turn snow,
> a sheer, bare cliff, outranging sight,
> brooding alone, aloft,
> Down I would hurl myself, deep down,
> and only the eagles would see.

The metaphor is necessary to poetic diction, and when language is denuded of metaphors dramatic tragedy dies—it is always thus. The cycle is seen in the works of Aeschylus through Euripides, in Shakespeare through Shirley.

The Greek and the Elizabethan used metaphors quite differently. The Greeks were content with recognizing the beauty inherent in an object, they did not feel the need of allowing the fancy too free a rein once the beautiful object was noted. Mention was almost enough; thereafter the beauty was evoked in the mind of the auditor: bright honey, salt wave, golden tresses, light wind, meadow grass. . . .[5]

Yet, granting this difference, Professor Hamilton's deduction does not necessarily follow. She writes: "The Greek poet lifts one corner of the curtain only. A glimpse is given, no more, but by it the mind is fired to see itself what lies behind. . . . Pindar takes two lovers to the door of their chamber and dismisses them: 'Secret are wise persuasion's keys unto love's sanctities.' This is not Shakespeare's way with Romeo and Juliet. The English method is to fill the mind with beauty; the Greek method was to set the mind to work." [6] This is an unfortunate generalization. Shakespeare did "fill the mind with beauty," to the extent that to listen with a half awareness to Shakespeare's lines is to feel half benumbed, like Caliban on the island:

> Sounds and sweet airs, that give delight, and hurt
> not.

[5] See Hamilton, *The Greek Way*, 62–77.
[6] *Ibid.*, 77.

Sometimes a thousand twangling instruments
Will hum about mine ears; and sometimes voices,
That if I then had waked after long sleep,
Will make me sleep again; and then, in dreaming,
The clouds methought would open, and show riches
Ready to drop upon me; that, when I waked,
I cried to dream again.

But that is not all. A goodly portion of Shakespeare's tragedies contain metaphysical lines—ironic observations, ambiguities in meaning, puns, ugly images, new and startling metaphors—that awaken the mind and hasten understanding. The music of the verse makes the understanding an emotional experience itself. Let us consider first the poetry of exclusion in Renaissance tragedy, and reserve, temporarily, the poetry of synthesis.

It is difficult, and perhaps impossible, to isolate the elements that merge in the diction of poetic tragedy. Ignoring the metaphysical elements for the moment, we can find several influences all but inextricably related by the time that Shakespeare and Chapman wrote. There is no need to underscore the notation that the Tudor and Jacobean world loved melody. Quite naturally Elizabethan tragedians consciously used stirring speech rhythms to move their audiences. Marlowe was the first to do this successfully. Secondly, a long series of effective metrical tragedies had given the tragedian a vocabulary that was invaluable for creating an atmosphere in which terror and horror were unavoidable emotions. Lastly, a profusion in speech (largely metaphors), the natural counterpart to other artistic expressions in a society that loved diffuseness, was used to shed new shafts of light on age-old themes.

Marlowe limited himself to "poetic oratory." (His "mighty line" is the *sine qua non* of Renaissance scholars.) Peele, as well as Marlowe, used the rhetoric of decorous declamation, and, again like Marlowe, used the rhythms of stately melody. Kyd, and others of the revenge tragedy writers, selected terms that are suggestive of an imagined nether world. The nature of the metaphors used by various dramatists differed noticeably, as Eliot points out below. But excluding the metaphysical elements of, say, Shakespeare and Chapman, there is a common purpose behind these techniques: to stir, and thoroughly, the emotions of the audiences. Horror was the objective.

"It is pertinent, at least to remark that Marlowe's 'rhetoric' is not, or not characteristically, Shakespeare's rhetoric; that Marlowe's rhetoric consists in a pretty simple huffle-snuffle bombast, while Shakespeare's is more exactly a vice of style, a tortured perverse ingenuity of images which dissipates instead of concentrating the imagination, and which may be due in part to influences by which Marlowe was untouched." [7] One influence that touched Marlowe (and this may be shown in lines borrowed) was Spenser's poetry. Marlowe borrowed from the master of melody. His purpose was to infuse music into imagery that was aesthetically pleasing and emotionally moving.

The musical element in poetry of exclusion is most important. Kenneth Burke has had Duke Orsino analyze his own speeches.[8] The questing mind behind metaphysical verse is not to be found in Orsino, or in the kind of poetry he symbolizes.

If music be the food of love, play on . . .

"As cells absorbing sunlight, as the fetus basking in its womb-heaven, *receiving* nutriment; not

[7] *Selected Essays*, 119.

[8] *Philosophy of Literary Form*, 344–349.

venturing forth aggressively, predaciously, as with those jungle animals that stalk, leap and capture before they eat, and thus do hating and injuring —but simply as larvae feed, let me take in gentle music." One key word is *receiving,* another key idea is found in *gentle music.*

> That strain again! it had a dying fall.

There is an implied wish in the language of Orsino: by excluding harshness in any form and by listening to repeated strains of music he would protect himself. He would become "a living nothing." Orsino, like Marlowe, knew how to shift from music to imagery, how, rather to synthesize them, and thus to add another sensuous pleasure:

> O, it came o'er my ear like the sweet sound,
> That breathes upon a bank of violets,
> Stealing and giving odour. . . .

From musical strains to banks of flowers to sweet smelling scents. The poet pulls the stops on the organ—and there are many sounds he consciously avoids.

A recent writer has given considerable attention to the "heroic medium" of Elizabethan tragedy.[9] He is concerned with showing that "Blank Verse . . . has its roots in medieval poetry." And his treatment is convincing. We learn that Surrey, Grimald, Norton, Gascoigne, Peele, Kyd and others experimented with balanced iambic lines, and that the diction of Marlowe rested on an established tradition. It is to oversimplify and to overglorify to give unbounded credit to Marlowe, as too many critics have done. Kyd, to select but one Shakespearean predecessor, wrote lines that were scarcely of less value to the maturing Shakespeare. His language, studded with images and words from the metrical tragedies, creates an atmosphere that is often re-created in the period of high tragedy:

Where shall I run to breathe my woes . . . ?
The blustering winds, conspiring with my words,
At my lament have moved the leafless trees,
Disrob'd the meadows of their flower'd green, . . .
Yet still tormented is my tortured soul
With broken sighs and restless passions,
That, winged, mount; and, hovering in the air,
Beat at the window of the brightest heavens,
Soliciting for justice and revenge. . . .

[9] Howard Baker, *Induction to Tragedy*, 48–106.

Chapman uses this diction inherited from the metrical tragedies, although he does not depend solely upon it.

> Languishing winds, and murmuring falls of waters,
> Sadness of heart and ominous secureness,
> Enchantments, dead sleeps, all the friends of rest,
> . . . make the violent wheels
> Of Time and Fortune stand. . . .

A careful reader of many of the revenge tragedies will turn up many such lines. Other influences have come in, and are often of equal importance, but the basic tone remains. The words are almost inevitable: justice, revenge, doleful, leafless, winds, lament, blustering, chill, pale, dread, stormy, deep, sleep, sobbing, and hundreds more. The mood is that of Sackville's *Induction;* the method is that of the carefully selective poet. Another, equally important technique of the tragedian, was to make his audience conscious of atmosphere by deluging them in words that were, cumulatively, suggestive of the desired atmosphere. Shakespeare's world loved detail. Its inheritance was Gothic, medieval. To ape the Greek way of writing (presuming they understood the nature of Greek style) would have been to deny that heritage. The elaborate costumes of lady and courtier, the chains of wrought gold, the decorated pendants, intricate jeweled boxes—these were the delights of Shakespeare's world. The Gothic cathedral, the illuminated manuscript, the stained glass windows, the elaborate ceremonies of the church—these had left their common mark on the mind of the Renaissance. Petrarchan conceits, euphuistic elaborations, Arcadian rhetoric—these dictated, in part, the nature of poetic diction. Just to read the title of their collections is to have proof that Elizabethans loved words. One of Dekker's titles is *The Fifteen Comforts of Rash and Inconsiderate Marriage; or, Select Animadversions upon the Miscarriages of a Wedded State*. Elizabethan poetic diction was built up by the same type of word-loving minds.

The diffuseness of Elizabethan poetry was also directly the result of the intellectual ferment of the sixteenth century. Authors in Shakespeare's generation and slightly earlier were aware that language was changing. John Cheke, who wrote the first piece of criticism in the English Renaissance, asked that the Englishman's language remain as isolated as his island. Otherwise, he implies, confusion will overtake language. But Niagara is not to be reasoned with: the flow of words from a distant classical world, the flow from a not-so-distant Italy and an even closer France threatened to choke the stream of English poetry. Some scholars tell us that English words doubled in number in the course of one hundred years. Some of the more pestiferous words lived the short span of an insect and disappeared. Professor Frederick W. Bateson draws a novel but apparently sound inference from these facts.[10] Poets "had an uneasy feeling all the time that their vocabulary was slipping away from under them, and, suspecting and distrusting it, they did not dare to confide the whole of their meaning to a single word or phrase. . . . And so they reinforced their primary meanings with repetitions, glosses, and amplifications. A shower of words and images splashes the reader's face." Copiousness and ornateness, brought about by "amplification," was a standard technique in writing.

The fear that meaning would soon be lost in a welter and flux of words passed eventually. By 1590 there was a conscious effort to use these new words in as many contexts as the mind could in-

[10] *English Poetry and the English Language.*

vent. The result of this open-hearted acceptance of new words is obvious: connotation, rather than denotation, was fast becoming the method of Elizabethan poets. Ambiguity was king. But this is another theme, one we shall take up shortly. Here we shall emphasize only these comments: *Profusion* is a key word in characterizing Elizabethan poetry. Fancy was allowed to play upon a theme, and fanciful were the lines that occurred to the poet. In the hands of the poet an abundant vocabulary often became a rapidly turning kaleidoscope, and sometimes the individual word becomes lost in the whirl of the unwinding poem.[11] Richard II is, like many of his fellow creations, unable to say a relatively simple thing in a simple way:

> How sour sweet music is
> When time is broke and no proportion kept!
> So is it in the music of men's lives.

[11] Yet to go as far as Bateson does, to say that "'Pure' prose is entirely a matter of ideas; 'pure' poetry is entirely a matter of phrases" is to invite a justified ridicule for the poet, and to oversimplify a complicated subject. Further, to say "drama, including poetic drama, is essentially a form of prose because its *media* are not words but ideas" is to deny that pure tragedy is poetic, and to ignore the fact that poetic tragedy is a composite usually of three types of writing: the direct communicative language of prose, the suggestive and connotative language of metaphysical verse, and the innately beautiful and musical quality of many denotative verses.

And here have I the daintiness of ear
To check time broke in a disorder'd string;
But for the concord of my state and time
Had not an ear to hear my true time broke.
I wasted time, and now doth Time waste me,—
My thoughts are minutes; and with sighs they jar
Their watches on unto mine eyes, the outward
 watch,
Whereto my finger, like a dial's point,
Is pointing still, in cleansing them from tears.

And sometimes other poets indicate a mastery of blank verse, of telling metaphors, of comparisons, of images that become wedded to the reader's mind. Hear De Flores of Middleton's *The Changeling:*

Can you weep Fate from its determined purpose?
So soon may you weep me.

No comparison could better suggest the inexorable will of De Flores. Or give ear to the Bussy of Chapman:

Man is a torch borne in the wind; a dream
But of a shadow, summ'd with all his substance;
And as great seamen, using all their wealth

> And skills in Neptune's deep invisible paths
> In tall ships richly built and ribb'd with brass,
> To put a girdle round about the world. . . .

Here there seem to be echoes from Shakespeare, some of whose warmth has escaped, but the rhetoric is out of the current feeling for language.

The late seventeenth century came to dislike Elizabethan poetry, which, Dryden said, was "pestered with figurative expression." In late Jacobean drama, one discovers, the delight in words has died. The plain, easily understood word and the abstraction—the prosaic—have overtaken drama. The language is all surface. They are the same words used by Shakespeare, but how differently they are ordered by Ford's pen:

> Tempt not the stars; young man, thou canst not
> play
> With the severity of fate: this change
> Of habit and disguise in outward view
> Hides not the secrets of thy soul within thee. . . .

Idea becomes of more importance than does the communication of an idea with which strong feeling is intimately related. While this is happening prose is becoming the vehicle of drama.

The Romantic poets, like their equally wrong eighteenth century predecessors, rigidly limited their visions: they demanded simplicity. This simplicity became the basis of Victorian harmony, the age's sense of "knowing." This temper of the Victorian era made its poetry what it is. The poetry of the nineteenth century was characterized by vagueness. A romantic haze hangs over much of it and the intellectual pith is soft, mushy; it lacks hardness, intensity. Even Browning, who prided himself on having hard kernels in his poems, often spreads out his thoughts like Donne's gold leaf:

"Gold, friends, repute, I left for him, I find
In him, why should I leave him then for gold,
Repute or friends?"—and you have felt your heart
Respond to such poor outcasts of the world
As to so many friends; bad as you please,
You've felt they were God's men and women still,
So, not to be disowned by you. But she
That stands there, calmly gives her lover up
As means to wed the Earl that she may hide
Their intercourse the surelier. . . .

And so, interminably. Actually such poetic diction is a packing of alternate (or four out of five) rifts with prose,—as though the mind were not capable of entertaining connotative, suggestive words or complex thoughts.

The next step—this one, upwards—was made by a new group of exclusionist poets. Most notable among them was Housman. There is no thickness in his imagery, no essentially functional necessity in his metaphors, no truly teasing quality in his words. The reason is easily got at: he has a simple proposition to make; the wax-polished, bright red apple is, he will have you discover, mushy, not at all what it seemed. Housman is a romantic ironist, and has won acclaim from an age that has glorified despair. He has, to a slight extent, helped to release poetry from the diction of the nineteenth century, and for that we must be grateful to him. Yet, we do not have to praise the lack of sincerity in his conscious pathos:

> Aye, lad, I lie easy,
>   I lie as lads would choose;
> I cheer a dead man's sweetheart.
>   Never ask me whose.

E. A. Robinson, like A. E. Housman before him, knew the things he wanted to say, and said them clearly in verse form. Nor was he impeded by the poetic machinery of the Victorian world. His diction however is, for the most part, that of the clear-thinking, facile prose writer.

> Cliff Klingenhagen had me in to dine
> With him one day; and after soup and meat,
> And all the other things there were to eat,
> Cliff took two glasses and filled one with wine
> And one with wormwood.

He does not sufficiently tease the reader's mind. Yet his blank verse is rhythmical with the deep cadences of the speaker whose strength of voice has mellowed as he has learned daily to appreciate the irony in exaggerated statements:

> He treads through Time's old wilderness
> As if the tramp of all the centuries
> Had left no roads—and there are *none* for him;
> He doesn't see them even with those eyes—
> And that's the pity, or I say it is.

Again, he can create an atmosphere of Celtic twilights in which a reader can become wilfully lost. Robinson proved that blank verse is possible in our idiom. He has belied Lucas' comment, that "If blank verse is good, it seems mock Elizabethan; and if it is bad, it is frightful." Much "mock-Elizabethan" contemporary blank verse—such as Anderson's cry to the "bright ironical gods"—is frightful, but there definitely is good blank verse that is quite distinct from that of the Elizabethans. We need now a tragedian who understands our heritage, who knows the metaphors that help understanding to blossom in the collective mind of the audience. The new tragedian will understand our heritage of debunking, the implications of the word "modern," American jargon,—our cast of thought and our idiom. We know the lowering bomber in its dive, the quickly flickering pictures on the screen, the sun setting through the haze of city smoke, the concrete road racing over hills and around clumps of trees, the slowly thumping scow in the harbor—these and thousands of similar images will not seem buttery in the Victorian way, or "phoney" in futile imitation of the Elizabethan's best. We can hear the lilting poetic prose of Synge and parts of Paul Vincent Carroll without writhing uncomfortably: their language sings. The foreign settings prepare us to accept a "foreign" language. We need a tragedian who knows our idiom.

Dialect differences are sufficiently great that we

can have "foreign" settings for plays within our own country. The rhythms of the speech, the locally suggested metaphor of a hundred varied settings can appeal forcefully to us. (The poet should be careful, however, not to exploit a region at the expense of his drama.) Lynn Riggs, in *Green Grow the Lilacs,* has written passages that approach poetry. Descriptive writing alone is not sufficient for drama of course (and Riggs has made no effort to portray inner struggle), but the images are vivid indications of the mind, the temper, the *milieu* in which the play is set:

Outside, the sun's jist crazy 'th the heat, beatin' on the prairie and the corn stalks. Passed a field in the bottom this mornin' whur the backwater had been. Ground all cracked, and blistered and bakin' in the sun. . . . The crawfish put up their pinchers and hustled about, 'cause their holes is all gone dry. . . . The crows went to honkin' at me when I rode th'ough the Dog Crick timber, and I could see hundreds of squirrels friskin' in the blackjacks.

Occasionally Anderson writes lines that could come only from the twentieth century. Mio is describing the execution of his father:

That night the guards,
walking in the flood-lights brighter than high noon,
led him between them with his trousers slit
and a shaven head for the cathodes. This sleet and
rain
that I feel cold here on my face and hands
will find him under thirteen years of clay
in prison ground.

There are some few lines in *Mary of Scotland* that are poetry, but generally Anderson's attempts fall pathetically short. Even though Anderson had greater technical ability as a poet, he would fail to write poetic tragedy. First, let us hear his own remarks on the nature of poetic tragedy.

In a note on poetry in contemporary drama Maxwell Anderson says our era is getting ready for a "consideration of man's place and destiny in prophetic rather than prosaic terms." Behind this remark is his belief that a new faith—the shape of which is as yet unknown—will fire men; for most discussions of the immediate facts of political, social, and economic life are themes of impermanence. Whatever the new faith, its expression must be poetic. And this implies that we must produce a dramatic poet comparable at least to the great of Greece and Elizabethan England. Ineluctably, poetic diction is allied to the dramatist's philosophical pattern. If his "vision" is a simple one, his poetry will reflect it—and his poetry will ring false. Whether or not America is ready to produce a tragedian is yet to be proved. We have poets with "mind," which prevents their singing lyrical nothings about the nobility of man, and we have poets who wear blinkers and therefore sing loud songs of hope. The two states of minds must be wedded. It seems reasonable to suppose that a tragedian, if one is to arise, will come from the former group, the poets who have sufficient intellectual integrity to refuse to propagandize in verse.

III

"The classic tendency," Frye writes, "is towards classification and concentration. And finally, in this instinct for transparency and definition, and in the consequent avoidance of whatever is vague and diffuse, the classic pretends to convey no more than lies within the ability of the author to understand or the power of language to represent; it is expressive, not suggestive." [12] Life to the Greek

[12] *Romance and Tragedy,* 338.

thinker might have been painful, but it was relatively simple. Let us hear Frye on the matter: "In the first place, modern life—to give the word *modern* its fullest extension as including whatever is novel to antiquity—is tremendously more complicated than ancient life ever was; and in the second place, our manner of looking at life has changed tremendously, to take no account of the advantage the Greek had over all other races in clarity of mind and penetration of vision. Consider, for one thing, how little the ancient knew as compared even with the contemporaries of Shakespeare, how small his stock of information. He was acquainted only with an infinitesimal portion of the universe; of the globe on which he walked he knew only an insignificant corner bordering on the Mediterranean Sea. He had by no means discovered all that the naked eye was capable of discovering, if properly used, to say nothing of that vast accumulation of fact which has been added to modern discovery by microscope and telescope and one another ingenious contrivance for the multiplication and extension of the senses."

The intention behind a Greek tragedy is usually quite apparent; that of the Shakespearean tragedies is questionable, puzzling. Witness the confusion of the Shakespearean critics. Sophocles, classical scholars tell us, was concerned, as were his high-minded fellows, with two most important concepts—happiness and justice. "Happiness and righteousness, he seems to think, are somehow paired together in the constitution of the cosmos, so that the former exists in some manner by virtue of the latter." This doctrine may offer complexities of a sort, but the consolation is great: there is a moral core to the universe. The Renaissance was not to destroy this faith; but the new complexities made faith in man's ability to get at that core more difficult to accept. Life quite suddenly began to explode. We see an extension of the idea today in the theory of the expanding universe. And we have the advantage of having been born into a world that accepts, although it rarely considers, the limitless expanse of the universe. In Shakespeare's day medievalism—at the heart of which was order and authority—was breaking up. It was becoming increasingly hard to believe in a moral universe, but the very fact that tragedy exists in the Renaissance is adequate proof that hope was not abandoned. To Sophocles, the moral doctrine was the thing; to Shakespeare, almost the enigma was the thing. A prosaic paraphrase—one hardly understandable to Shakespeare, but a logical outgrowth of the world in *King Lear* might read:

> Events are variables.
> In our going, as in our coming thither
> Relativity is all.

The Renaissance poet with insight saw five roads where Sophocles saw one. Perhaps Macbeth's speech is symbolic of the confusion:

> Who can be wise, amazed, temperate and furious
> Loyal and neutral, in a moment?

Shakespeare reflects, particularly in his more inscrutable plays, this incongruity. Quite naturally, his poetry will possess ambiguities, even as his characters; his integrity as an artist will cause him to offer only limited interpretations within the confusion. His language, therefore, will be composed of the diction of ordinary speech—puns, vulgarisms, ironies, word play. He will attain to the sublime, on occasion, but it will be the "sublime" of Longinus, not of Dr. Johnson.

In regard to irony, I venture a generalization. The reason that the Greeks were not so much concerned with irony—Aristotle mentions it but once in the *Poetics*—was that life did not seem as ironic to Sophocles as it did to Shakespeare, who saw more variables. True, dramatic irony is Greek. But dramatic irony is relatively simple. The audience knows more than the tragic hero, and therefore can appreciate the irony present in some of the hero's statements. A step further has been taken by the Renaissance tragedian: the tragic hero himself is aware of basic incongruities. "And be these juggling fiends no more believed," says Macbeth,

> That palter with us in a double sense;
> That keep the word of promise to our ear
> And break it to our hope.

An aspect of the tragic hero's introspections, his struggling to understand the cosmos, is his eventual consciousness of irony. In each age the *modern* men are those who rise, ever so slightly, above the great sea of pristine unconsciousness. For this there is a reward or a penalty, depending upon the viewpoint. The audience of a tragedy are in a superb position—with their knowledge that is temporarily greater than that of the stage characters

—to smile ironically, and perhaps smugly, as they watch a noble but fallible creature carefully building a house of cards. With its greater perspective the audience sees in what spot the wall will give way. But if the tragic hero were so obtuse that the irony of his downfall never struck him there would be no tragedy from a modern's viewpoint, because there would be no understanding. Here, however, we are concerned not with the audience, but with the tragic hero. His awareness of the irony of his life comes a bit later than that of the audience, but his ultimate consciousness of it is far more intense. He sees that the seemingly orderly system which once appeared so easy to control has an imp at the switch. He comes to knowledge at the price of profound sorrow. Obviously when the tragic hero recognizes the jarring differences between the world he envisioned and the world he finds, he is moved to draw together the world of the might-have-been and the world-that-is into a common unity in his consciousness.

"The ironist," one writer tells us, "looks more deeply than most men into the laws of cause and effect and of unconscious motivation. . . . He therefore finds ways of extricating himself from the normal, or vulgar point of view with its fatal limitations."[13] The tragic hero finds himself in the center of a series of situations that, viewed objectively, teaches one a considerable lot about man's relative unimportance in the cosmos. Setting emotion aside, the tragic hero surveys the circumstances that are crushing the life from him and coolly comments on the forces at work. He becomes temporarily a spectator at his own catastrophe. The scene itself is fascinating, and the personal element recedes. Consider Hamlet's leave-taking of Horatio, or note Othello's of Lodovico:

When you shall these unlucky deeds relate,
Speak of me as I am; nothing extenuate,—
Nor set down aught in malice: then must you speak
Of one that lov'd not wisely but too well;
Of one not easily jealous, but, being wrought,
Perplex'd in the extreme; of one whose hand,
Like the base Indian, threw a pearl away
Richer than all his tribe. . . .

This is the intellectual evaluation of his own tragedy. Look on me, Othello seems to say, and learn the irony of having these virtues that we are told

[13] David Worcester, *The Art of Satire*, 139.

lead to happiness and good living. We have been misinformed.

This *awareness* is a prerequisite to the writing of metaphysical poetry and also dramatic tragedy. In fact, one critic, Mark Van Doren, has defined metaphysical poetry in such a way that he might be describing the basis of irony. Metaphysical poetry, he says, may be figuratively illustrated by the letter Y. One arm of the letter represents wit, the other seriousness. Today we have the concepts in mind as both divorced and antithetical, at least in our poetry. (This is not quite true, as Professor H. W. Wells and Professor Cleanth Brooks have shown.) Whereas in the seventeenth century the poet's work was conceived at the base of the Y, that is, poetry was at once witty (not necessarily "funny") and serious. Irony, which serves to reconcile discordant attitudes and beliefs, is at the very heart of metaphysical poetry.

We will note one thing in recalling the language of Kyd: he is concerned with the analysis of Hieronimo's emotion. Unfortunately he does not probe deeply. Allen Tate in his "A Note on Elizabethan Satire" says that Elizabethan satirists were the first to step out from the allegorical stream, in which an interpretation of man's life seemed a relatively simple problem. Tate notes that Wyatt is among the first of the antiallegorical poets, those in whose language may be seen "the strain between images and rhythm, opposites 'yoked by violence together,' in varying degrees of violence." Tate might have given attention to metaphysical lines in the dramatic tragedies. The language was the child of its age.

The nature of man, once the theology of the medieval system was put aside, was seen as complex. Man was not good, he was not evil: he was human. And he was difficult to understand. It was not sufficient—to the contrary, it was stacking the cards—to pass off a group of simple allegorical figures as the means of understanding the evil resident in man. Let us use Tate's words: "The allegorical symbol is constant and homogeneous, like the Red Cross Knight; the richer, poetic symbol, like Prospero, does not invite the oversimplification of certain of its qualities, but asks to be taken in all its manifold richness."

Alan Swallow in "Induction as Poetic Method" [14] is concerned with the reasons behind this phe-

[14] *New Mexico Review* (Aug., 1941), 267–276.

nomenon: why was the medieval world more concerned with "generalized experience in poetry" whereas the Renaissance poet often is concerned with rendering an individual psychological "experience fully and precisely"? The answer, this critic says, is in the philosophical patterns of the two periods. The Renaissance poet abandoned deductive and illustrative logic and turned to experience itself, from which he inductively sought his answers. The latter technique meant that the Renaissance poet would turn to actual experiences, to sensations themselves. And personal experiences are complex. Edgar says of Lear:

> . . . his flaw'd heart,—
> 'Twixt two extremes of passion, joy and grief,
> Burst smilingly.

This matter of synthesis in poetry is intimately related to an artist's integrity, and his integrity is intimately related to his honest portrayal of character. The moralizer or the propagandist—and there is something of both in each—is essentially dishonest. Shakespeare, it seems to me, was neither. Let us recall Professor George Lyman Kittredge's interpretation of Claudius, for in it we are reminded of Shakespeare's refusal to gild the lily. Many actors and critics have made Claudius "a cross between Uriah Heep and the villain of melodrama." The character of Shakespeare is "a born ruler of men," one who could sympathize with "poor Ophelia," one who could face damnation and yet remain "so pitilessly honest" that he could not pray for forgiveness. He is the same man who could, in "lawless love for his brother's crown and his brother's wife, [creep] into the garden with juice of cursed hebenon in a vial. . . . Here is no inconsistency, but harmonious synthesis of discordant elements. We have a man before us—a very great man, though an enormous malefactor." [15] Another very capable Renaissance scholar has given warning that when a man seems inconsistent he seems so only because the observer lacks some of the facts. This discussion of character may seem to be a digression. Actually it is another view of the same urn. The poet who synthesizes has truth on his side, as does the dramatist who refuses to create types. The tragedian must give an honest portrayal of the tragic experience; to do so he must not exclude seeming incongruities. His poetry will reflect the seeming incongruities. The

[15] *Shakespere,* 42–43.

tragedian is a poet of insight, not a dreamer of pleasant dreams. Shakespeare would have agreed with this:

> The poet and the dreamer are distinct,
> Diverse, sheer opposite, antipodes.

To use a metaphor, the tragedy is the macrocosm, the poetic language the microcosm. Young Romeo's words and phrases are ignited questions, flinted from his mind:

> I'll bury thee in a triumphant grave;
> A grave? . . .
> . . . .
> Shall I believe
> That unsubstantial death is amorous,
> And that the lean abhorred monster keeps
> Thee here in the dark to be his paramour?

It should be apparent that the language of the tragic character has aspects in common with the language of metaphysical poets. To quote Professor Brooks, "There are, in these [metaphysical] poems, the swift, abrupt openings; there are the sudden shifts of tone. There is the use of shock, and the sudden turn of thought which leads to an unexpected climax. To turn to deeper and more significant characteristics, the poet's approach to any given subject, however abstract or general it may be, is always made through some concrete situation . . . they are attempts made by the poet to explore."

The metaphors the tragedian uses, if they are to awaken one mentally, must be composed of elements that are divergent in the extreme. This is a line from *Bussy d'Ambois,*

> . . . life['s] nothing but a courtier's breath.

A moment's consideration tells us that the comparison is an apt one. Still he is not satisfied that the audience understands, so Bussy probes into his mind again.

> Nothing is made of nought, of all things made,
> Their abstract being a dream but of a shade.

Then, with death upon him, he struggles for one last moment of coupled thought and feeling.

> My sun is turn'd to blood, in whose red beams
> Pindus and Ossa, hid in drifts of snow

Laid on my heart and liver, from their veins
Melt like two hungry torrents, eating rocks
Into the ocean of all human life,
And make it bitter, only with my blood.

The pun, so dear to Elizabethan and Jacobean poets, is so obviously a part of the tragedian's poetic diction that the point does not have to be labored. (Current appreciation of puns is lessened by our artificial and feigned dislike of word play.) How intense must have been the appreciation of Shakespeare's audience when Romeo punned on the verb "to die." Professor Brooks has made the point in these words: "[Prescott] . . . shows that the verb 'to die' was used in the seventeenth century with the meaning 'to experience the consummation of the sexual act,' and suggests that there is a shade of the meaning latent in

Juliet. Yea, noise?—then I'll be brief.—O happy dagger!
[*Snatching Romeo's dagger*]
This is thy sheath; [*Stabs herself*] there rust,
and let me die. [*Falls on Romeo's body and dies.*]

. . . Indeed the whole tragedy of love and death is summed up in this last word and corresponding last action" of Juliet.[16] Very definitely this pun serves to reconcile discordant elements: Juliet's hope and Juliet's intellectual appreciation of the futility of hope.

Shakespeare did not shy away from the pun on "to die" because in a tragedy the pruderies, the pretenses of life are ripped and shredded. It is one thing to be wilfully vulgar, to consciously ignore man's dignity, it is another thing to sidestep actualities, to use ornamental language when the "vulgar idiom" is natural and more expressive. Dr. Johnson disliked "the blanket of dark"; he must have despised Hamlet's

> I'll lug the guts into the neighbour room.

Consider, too, the poetic expressiveness in Othello's saying:

> I had rather be a toad,
> And live upon the vapour of a dungeon,

[16] *Modern Poetry and the Tradition,* 27. Brooks considers this also in his article in *The Language of Poetry*. Professor John Olive points out what seems to me a fine illustration in *The Spanish Tragedy,* II, iv, 30–48.

Than keep a corner in the thing I love
For others' uses.

Othello's metaphor is metaphysical in that the toad image is not pretty or elegant; it was not conceived with the ideal of "high seriousness" in mind. Shakespeare was aware that to exclude figures that are not innately lovely was to cut out a large area of poetic experience. In one of the most powerful passages in his complete work Shakespeare culminated a series of relatively commonplace images with two that are ugly, depressing:

Tomorrow, and tomorrow, and tomorrow,
Creeps in this petty pace from day to day,
To the last syllable of recorded time;
And all our yesterdays have lighted fools
The way to dusty death. Out, out, brief candle;
Life's but a walking shadow, a poor player,
That struts and frets his hour upon the stage,
And then is heard no more; it is a tale
Told by an idiot, full of sound and fury,
Signifying nothing.

Richards has said this: "Tragedy is perhaps the most general, all-accepting, all-ordering experience known. It can take anything into its organisation, modifying it so that it finds a place." Surely Shakespeare's diction is an aid in creating the "all-ordering, all-accepting" mood in audience. It is inconceivable that poetic tragedy in the modern world can be written without employing metaphysical poetry.

The long interim between Elizabethan tragedy and the now fading naturalism has seen curious bypaths for poetry. Child of a scientific-minded world, the poet has examined rationalism, has reacted from that and turned to the artificiality of unreachable hopes, has again reacted and mired himself in naturalism, and has moved once more toward poetry of the intellect. These channels cannot be examined here. We can simply state that such an ex-arch cynic as Huxley seems now prepared to take the tragic view; yes, and Eliot. The future is not quite clear. At least we can look at the present.

Eliot, of course, knows that to simplify a concept is to state a partial truth. Agatha, in *The Family Reunion,* gives voice to many of his insights:

Liberty is a different kind of pain from prison. . . .
In a world of fugitives
The person taking the opposite direction
Will appear to run away. . . .

Harry and the Chorus express others. The evil that Harry feels and senses about him is frozen into such a line as this,

> You all look so withered and young.

This is poetry worthy of a place in dramatic tragedy. Perhaps, however, our emotional reactions could have been intensified if Eliot had further freed his Muse: she might have created a lighter mood, a refulgence of bright words, of provocative images, of stirring rhythms, and moving melodies.

The only other writer of dramatic poetry to approach—or possibly surpass—Eliot's work is Yeats. In a sense, Yeats held a view of existence, and possessed the inclinations and talents as a poet, prerequisite to the writing of dramatic tragedy.

In his poems "I am of Ireland" and "After Long Silence," Yeats presents his view of tragedy. He speaks frequently of the heroic affirmation, of victory in defeat—the tragic view. Oddly, this view does not find expression in his dramas. We have the brief comments of his that "the day of tragedy will return slowly" and that "We begin to live when we have conceived life as tragedy." The former statement is not elaborated. If it were we might have the explanation of Yeats' failure to attempt a dramatic tragedy. There is a lesson in his poetry however—one that would indicate that conceivably he might have been *the* contemporary poet to bring tragedy back to the contemporary stage. The implications can be seen in a brief rehearsal of his poetic development.

We may select such words as these from his early poetry: *shadowy, grey, dim, sigh, desolate, pale, wan, foam, flame;* with these we can contrast these from his later poetry: *rag, naked stone, insolent, ditch, fool, shriek,* and so on. The early poetry is "sensual music," the later poetry is too often "mere complexities." In "Sailing to Byzantium," however, the static, gold-packed rifts are not the sole strength of the poem; the emphasis shifts until the poet has expressed his keen awareness of the tragic view. The early lines begin:

The young
In one another's arms; birds in the trees,
—Those dying generations—at their song;
The salmon-falls, the mackerel-crowded seas. . . .

Some of the later lines are:

O sages standing in God's holy fire
As in the gold mosaic of a wall,
Come from the holy fire, perne in a gyre,
And be the singing-masters of my soul.
Consume my heart away; sick with desire
And fastened to a dying animal
It knows not what it is; and gather me
Into the artifice of eternity.[17]

Unfortunately the tragic view, so dear to Yeats, is not to be found in his dramas.

One can trace a gradual purging of ornament from his dramatic poetry. "The course of improvement," says Eliot, "is towards a greater and greater starkness. The beautiful line for its own sake is a luxury dangerous even for the poet who

[17] See *The Southern Review,* "William Butler Yeats Memorial Issue," VII (Winter, 1942), especially the articles by L. C. Knights, T. S. Eliot, F. O. Matthiessen.

has made himself a virtuoso of the technique of the theater. What is necessary is a beauty which shall not be in the line or isolable passage, but woven into the dramatic texture itself; so that you can hardly say whether the lines give grandeur to the drama, or whether it is the drama which turns words into poetry." There is,—admirable as Eliot's integrity here is—I think, a fallacy in this.

Not all speeches are necessary for furthering the dramatic action; the dramatist may, as Shakespeare does, pause to fill the air with poetry—poetry definitely "isolable" from "the dramatic texture." Certainly, as in *Purgatory,* to make excessive use of such stark lines—

> *Boy.* What education have you given me?
>
> *Old Man.* I gave you the education that befits
> A bastard that a pedlar got
> Upon a tinker's daughter in a ditch.
> When I had come to sixteen years old
> My father burned down the house when drunk.—

is only slightly more realistic than to spray the atmosphere with Celtic vapours from a world that never was:

> Finvarra, and their Land of Hearts' Desire,
> Where beauty has no ebb, decay no flood,
> But joy is wisdom, Time an endless song.

Even those speeches that do further the dramatic action should not be exclusively stark.

The nature of poetic diction in dramatic tragedy of the future—granting, of course, that the tragic view does not sidle off into the shadows again—may be quite impossible to predict. To expect a renewal of Elizabethan poetic diction is to ignore the obvious fact that language grows from the inner necessity of the poet, from his need to express his perception of the world he knows. The language of Elizabethans can be little more than a guide to the tragedian who will write tomorrow. Yet, knowing the complexities of Shakespearean diction we must, it seems, feel that the poets of twilights and misty, sun-lit vistas misinterpret our world only slightly less one-sidedly than those who, with Lawrence, see "the essence of poetry with us in this age of stark and unlovely actualities [as necessarily a language of] stark directness." The latter type of poetry can make us sickeningly aware of the evil in our minds and hearts but what of the language that will express the joy in tragedy? Though his plays do not reflect this particular belief, Yeats reminded us that "in Greece the tragic chorus danced." Perhaps there is a compromise to be found in the "sprung rhythm" of Auden, who hopes through this technique to "restore to poetry a wider social range." The sincere intellectualism of Yeats and Eliot has limited their audience. The lack of sincere, or at least adequate, intellectualism on the commercial stage has limited tragedy.

Coda: The Present and the Future

It is an unhappy circumstance that the contemporary theatre has so little to offer anyone who would examine the threads and discover the pattern of contemporary "tragedy." Ibsen is no longer pertinent, though his criticisms can still move us. Shaw is probably congenitally incapable of ever having discovered the tragic view. O'Neill, in his preoccupation with psychological theory and abnormal types has yet to do a play that transcends the transitory interests, however intense, of a generation. Even more deeply mired in the bog of naturalism were Gorki and Toller, among the Europeans. In America, Rice, polarized to the same cellarage, has never been able to write in the positive manner of tragedy. O'Casey, cynically brilliant and embittered, reflects only an effective negativism. Galsworthy's sensitivity and fairness give his work an air of considered morality and goodness—which has nothing to do with the crushing evil of universal forces. To dismiss the bulk of contemporary dramatists with a seemingly cavalier gesture is not unfair: until very recently no overtures have been made toward the tragic spirit.

Naturalism has threatened and threatens to destroy the self-sufficient individualism glorified by Sophocles and Shakespeare and Montaigne. The betrayal of the group by individualists in contemporary Europe has caused such a violent reaction against liberalism, against the faith in self-discipline that the opposite poles are arrived at: that only a collectivist society can be allowed to exist and that human nature is essentially base. Such cynicism is the heartbeat of naturalistic fiction and drama, as can be seen in the words of Hauptmann: "At a distance the world looks pretty enough. From near it's brainless, banal, and indecent beyond words." This, in large part, has been the theme of contemporary literature.

> To thine own self be true,
> And it must follow as the night the day,
> Thou canst not then be false to any man.

Largely this sentiment has obtained in all great

literature: without it nobility of spirit is inconceivable. But few contemporaries have been concerned with nobility. Consequently from being symbols of noble individualism contemporary protagonists have become symbols of pettiness, deceit, cynicism, lust, stupidity, and bestiality. Thus the keystone of dramatic tragedy was lost. The individual had prostituted himself to selfish interests. At least one, however, among the postwar "realists," the coauthor of *What Price Glory,* was anxious to preach a new faith and at the most propitious moment he did. Maxwell Anderson refuses to accept the "pathological defeatism" of the twenties.

This refusal of Anderson to degrade the individual is the result of his belief in the "inviolability of the human personality." The basis of his belief however is not, like Eliot's, that of neo-Catholicism; he is not attempting to "find" himself in the faith of his fathers—he seems to be an agnostic in all but his belief in human dignity. He harks back in spirit to Pico della Mirandola, but without the Christian platonism of the Italian. He is satisfied to find gleams of light in an occasional art work, in conscious reordering of social injustices—but particularly in self-dedication.

A man must die for what he believes . . . and if he won't, he'll end believing nothing at all—and that's death, too.

The words are King McCloud's, the sentiment is that of all of Anderson's "tragic" protagonists. In his *Essence of Tragedy,* Anderson says the same thing in a slightly different way: "The hero who is to make the central discovery in a play must have some variation of what Aristotle calls a tragic fault—and the reason he must have it is that when he makes his discovery he must change in himself and in his action." Once having discovered his "flaw" the protagonist must change his course. In his realization and consequent change of action the protagonist becomes noble: he becomes true to himself, and "it must follow. . . ."

Perhaps Robert Sherwood preceded Anderson by a year or so in giving the contemporary stage an "heroic morality play," in this instance a melodrama but driven by the same spirit of dedication. Alan Squier, the protagonist of *The Petrified Forest,* had sold himself to a wealthy art-loving woman who had seen a "major artist" in him. After his years of self-prostitution Squier hopes to find "something to believe in. I've been hoping to find something that's worth living for—and dying for." In Gabrielle, born of a French mother, who aches to leave the petrified forest and to study painting in France he finds the opportunity to sacrifice the husk his life has become. The payment upon his death of an insurance policy will give her five thousand dollars and her opportunity. He will cause the gangster Duke Mantee to shoot him. "I'm not going away anywhere . . . I've found the thing I was looking for—here, in the Valley of the Shadow." Anderson himself has pointed to the fact that Sherwood has created another hero of dedication in *Abe Lincoln in Illinois*. The discovery is made by Lincoln "that he has been a coward, that he has stayed out of the fight for the Union because he was afraid." This produces a "profound emotional effect" on Lincoln and "gives an entirely new direction to the play." Lincoln finally reached an understanding within himself, the realization that he could bring order out of chaos. In that realization he becomes noble. Sherwood, like Anderson, has continued to cause his plays to grow around the characters of protagonists who are willing to die that decency may live. *There Shall Be No Night*, regardless of the aspects of its current political implications, is important as an expression of Sherwood's faith; and in the preface to this play he has recalled that he has always been searching for reason to believe in man's eventual redemption as the inevitable surcease for a desperately frustrated people. In the death of Erik in this last play Sherwood sees a symbol "of man's unconquerable aspiration to dignity. . . ." Again the same faith is found in the words of Kaarlo: "We have within ourselves the power to conquer bestiality, not with our swords, but with the power of the light that is in our minds." There is more lustre to the phrases of Anderson; his message is the same as that of Sherwood.

It would seem that some of the most popular of the fiction writers and dramatists of the twenties, men who walked in the rain and felt sorry for themselves, men who believed in nothing and who delighted in drawing "a mustache and beard on the Mona Lisa" have felt the need of embracing this new faith. Even Hemingway (so far as the stage version may be his) offered us a character in *The Fifth Column* who awakens to the importance of giving his life to fighting against a vicious system.

This desire on the part of some contemporary

writers to correct the ills of society has resulted in a preoccupation with the evils inherent in specific ideologies—a legitimate and righteous interest. Unfortunately, however, the interpretations one gives certain of these ideologies depend largely on rapidly changing circumstances—on economic, political, and social conditions. Inevitably a sudden shift or change in a given situation can turn what seemed an apparent evil into an apparent good. Thus, for example, the seeming evil forces at work in *There Shall Be No Night* were seen to be, after a very short time, a temporary good. The political, social, or economic problem can win the emphasis away from a concern with irrevocable evil inherent in the nature of man and the universe. This statement is, in little, almost the entire history of the contemporary theatre.

Fortunately, some contemporary writers have striven to rise above even their concern over ideologies. In his latest work Hemingway gave even fuller statement to his change of heart. His newest, and likely his best, fictional hero, Robert Jordan, takes his place beside Tom Joad, Mio, Abraham Lincoln, and all heroes who, having been conquered, die unconquered. There is a brief hesitation, a moment in which the older spirit of the twenties comes in conflict with the new; Robert Jordan is soliloquizing as he lies under a tree on a Spanish battleground: "Don't get cynical. The time is too short and you have just sent her away. Each one does what he can. You can do nothing for yourself but perhaps you can do something for another." His act of faith follows: "I have fought for what I believed in for a year now. If we win here we will win everywhere. The world is a fine place and worth the fighting for and I hate very much to leave it. . . . You've had as good a life as any because of these last days. You do not want to complain when you have been so lucky. I wish there was some way to pass on what I've learned. Christ, I was learning fast there at the end." In the death of Robert Jordan the world sustains no inconsiderable loss: he has the capacity for understanding and seems, at his death, to have been approaching a state of mind where he can fathom the war and his part in it; he endures his suffering courageously for a single purpose, to kill another rebel soldier— "And if you wait and hold them up even a little while, or just get that officer, that may make all the difference. One thing well done can make. . . ." He has approached an understanding of the evil in his immediate world, he sees himself as a part of humanity; and the reader comes to know "for whom the bell tolls"—for humanity in him.

The self-dedication, however, of these protagonists—noble as they may be—is the very thing that keeps them from being tragic heroes. "Some people suppose that the sting of tragedy lies in the fact that the hero dies; whereas it lies in the fact that the hero is one inherently capable of choosing right, and yet, for reasons within or outside his control, chooses wrong when opportunity comes, and suffers for his mistake. In one's life opportunity comes once and never again and the past is irrevocable. If the hero chooses right, his death is no tragedy." [1] In this observation of Mr. Ritchie is one of the keys to Anderson's and Sherwood's and Hemingway's failure to write tragedy. Anderson in particular is wedded to the belief of the necessity for personal dedication. And he has been instrumental in winning other critics to his belief.[2] Anderson writes: "A play should lead up to and away from a central crisis, and this crisis should consist in a discovery by the leading character which has an indelible effect on his thought and

[1] A. D. Ritchie, *Philosophy of A. N. Whitehead,* 343.

[2] See Matthiessen, *American Renaissance,* 350.

emotion and completely alters his course of action. . . ." He then goes on to say that the protagonist recognizes his error and therefore changes his course of action. On the contrary, the tragic hero has the potentiality of choosing the right, or morally elevating course of action, but fails to see his error in time to change. "If the hero chooses right, his death is no tragedy." Regeneration—discussed by Aristotle in terms of the recognition scene—does have a place, and an important one, in the tragedy, but considerably later in the play than Anderson would have it. It comes after the fall of the tragic hero, after the sequence of events caused by his failure to see his fault have come all but full circle. The distinction can be seen more clearly in the following attempt to classify this new type of drama which the contemporary theatre is witnessing: "The variation of what Aristotle calls a tragic fault comes closer to what Jesus called a man's 'coming to himself' and to what the Church has called conversion. It is a painful but not a tragic event. I should like to suggest the name heroic morality play for [this] newly developed type of serious drama. . . ." [3]

Anderson's protagonists choose to die, even as

[3] Received in a letter from Merritt Y. Hughes.

the martyrs of the Christian church. To be unfair, one can say that Anderson formulates his philosophy in terms of Lloyd Douglas. Such plays have a religious rather than a tragic ending. They offer consolation in a dogma, not, primarily, in the strength of man. In so sidestepping, the dramatist loses an opportunity to write poetic lines of ecstatic intensity. In learning the futility of revenge Mio has answered the problem of his life:

> I've groped long enough
> through this everglades of old revenges—here
> the road ends. —Miriamne, Miriamne,
> the iron I wore so long—it's eaten through
> and fallen from me. . . .

Mio understands the emptiness of hatred; he is converted to the Christian view. His problem was answerable, and therefore hardly tragic.[4]

In considering these heroes of dedication one may think back to Eliot's Prufrock, the Hamlet of the twenties. "I have seen the moment of my greatness flicker," he said; but he could come to

[4] A rather full evaluation of Anderson's plays can be found in the following articles: (1) Vincent Wall, "Maxwell Anderson: The Last Anarchist," *Sewanee Review,* XLIX (July–Sept., 1941), 339–369; (2) Edward Foster, "Core of Belief," *ibid.,* L (Jan.–Mar., 1942), 87–100.

no decision, only a "hundred indecisions" and a "hundred visions and revisions." Even death had become cloaked in vulgarity and cheap pretense—

> And I have seen the eternal Footman hold my coat,
> and snicker,

He had moments of insight, but no sustained courage—

> . . . in short, I was afraid.

These failures in the human—indecision, debasement, cowardliness—have been turned in this new drama into the opposing virtues. And yet there is a simplicity to this new faith that, in the light of the great tragic ironists, one suspects will cause a strong unpleasant reaction, foreshadowings of which have already appeared.

We have already mentioned the work of contemporary metaphysical poets who have attempted to write tragedy. As a group, they contrast quite sharply with professional dramatists. Auden and Isherwood have failed to create a tragic hero who through his suffering and struggle develops a spiritual resiliency in which he is sufficient unto himself. Michael Ransom apparently fails to understand the forces that have destroyed him, and is, therefore, a pathetic symbol of an age that has failed to understand itself. Yeats has written no full length dramas, and the plays he has written are so ringed in symbolism, so consciously intellectual, that his meaning does not quite come through. Eliot, perhaps of all contemporaries the one best equipped to write tragedy, has chosen a pattern of supernaturalism that either we are not ready for or that is a retreat from the intensity of his own awareness of evil. At least these poets are not content to glorify man simply because they believe they should. A sense of basic incongruities —of evil intertwined with goodness, of hopes that mother ironies—is the pith of their thought. Mind, not sentiment, would seem to be the hope of the modern theatre. In Greece and in England when mind discovered spirit there was tragedy.